Alexander Hamilton
From Obscurity to Greatness

MAY 17 REC'D

WORD PORTRAITS OF AMERICA'S FOUNDERS

Alexander Hamilton
From Obscurity to Greatness

Compiled and Edited
by
John P. Kaminski

Published for
The Center for the Study of the American Constitution
by the

WISCONSIN HISTORICAL SOCIETY PRESS

Published by the Wisconsin Historical Society Press
Publishers since 1855

The Wisconsin Historical Society helps people connect to the past by collecting, preserving, and sharing stories. Founded in 1846, the Society is one of the nation's finest historical institutions.
Order books by phone toll free: (888) 999-1669
Order books online: shop.wisconsinhistory.org
Join the Wisconsin Historical Society: wisconsinhistory.org/membership

© 2016 by State Historical Society of Wisconsin

For permission to reuse material from *Alexander Hamilton: From Obscurity to Greatness* (ISBN 978-0-87020-803-4; e-book ISBN 978-0-87020-804-1), please access www.copyright.com or contact the Copyright Clearance Center, Inc. (CCC), 222 Rosewood Drive, Danvers, MA 01923, 978-750-8400. CCC is a not-for-profit organization that provides licenses and registration for a variety of users.

Cover painting: *Alexander Hamilton* by John Trumbull (1792), jointly owned by Crystal Bridges Museum of American Art and The Metropolitan Museum of Art, Gift of Credit Suisse, 2013; www.metmuseum.org

Printed in Canada
Cover design by Erin Kirk New

20 19 18 17 16   1 2 3 4 5

Library of Congress Cataloging-in-Publication Data
Names: Kaminski, John P., compiler, editor.
Title: Alexander Hamilton : from obscurity to greatness / compiled and edited by John P. Kaminski.
Description: Madison : Wisconsin Historical Society Press, 2016 | Series: Word portraits of America's founders | Includes bibliographical references and index.
Identifiers: LCCN 2016022480 | ISBN 9780870208034 (hardcover : alk. paper) | ISBN 9780870208041 (ebook)
Subjects: LCSH: Hamilton, Alexander, 1757–1804—Sources. | Statesmen—United States—Biography—Sources. | United States—Politics and government—1775–1783—Sources. | United States—Politics and government—1783–1809—Sources.
Classification: LCC E302.H2 A44 2016 | DDC 973.4092 [B]—dc23
LC record available at https://lccn.loc.gov/2016022480

♾ The paper used in this publication meets the minimum requirements of the American National Standard for Information Sciences—Permanence of Paper for Printed Library Materials, ANSI Z39.48-1992.

For Wauwatosa West High School
"We the People" Team
Perennial Wisconsin State Champion

Chad Mateske
Teacher

Thomas Schneck • Mark Young
Attorney Mentors

Aubrianna Mierow • Nicole Mystrow • Adam Fendos
Student Mentors

Contents

Preface ix
Introduction xiii

Descriptions of Alexander Hamilton   1

Hamilton's Descriptions of Others   83

Emblematic Quotations   163

Biographical Notes 205
Index 211
About the Author 221

Preface

During the last decades there has been a renewed interest in the Founding era of American history. A few general studies of the period, as well as a handful of biographies of George Washington, Thomas Jefferson, John Adams, Benjamin Franklin, and Alexander Hamilton, have captured the public's attention, spawning television mini-series and lately a Broadway play. A significant catalyst for this resurgence has been the publication of the Founders' papers in multi-volume series. Grants from the National Historical Publications and Records Commission, the National Endowment for the Humanities, and a few large and small foundations have supported the publication process. Several years ago, Edmund S. Morgan, Yale's productive and much-admired historian of early America, noted that the publication of the Founders' papers was the single greatest scholarly achievement of the twentieth century. For nearly half a century, I have been fortunate to share in this monumental effort to preserve and disseminate this critical part of the American historical, constitutional, and literary legacy.

Despite renewed interest in the Founders, Americans still know very little about this important generation. Textbooks, sometimes good and sometimes not, often relate only brief accounts of the Founders' public lives, rarely mentioning anything personal.

I have been reading the Founders' papers for many years—some of them in manuscript collections in libraries and historical societies, some in various kinds of microfiche, others in hundreds of incidental publications, such as journals or selective single volumes, and many in the ever-increasing number of volumes in NHPRC- and NEH-sponsored editions. Midway through this reading, I began compiling databases of quotations describing the thoughts and feelings of several of the Founders, including Washington, Jefferson, Thomas Paine, John Jay, Hamilton, and John and Abigail Adams. While mining the papers of John Adams, I began to compile a new database: the Founders' opinions of each other. In 2008, the University of Virginia Press published a selection of this database as *The Founders on the Founders: Word Portraits from the American Revolutionary Era,* which contained quotations describing thirty principal Founders. My database, which now consists of entries describing more than 450 people, has continued to grow.

The Wisconsin Historical Society Press has inaugurated a new series of volumes, each volume focused on a single Founder, drawing on this growing database of quotations. The quotations in each volume represent opinions of a particular Founder by contemporaries, and that Founder's opinions of his contemporaries. Quotations in which the subject assesses himself are also included, as well as "emblematic quotations." These final quotations are not self-reflections by the Founder, though they provide glimpses into the Founder's character and therefore can be viewed as semi-autobiographical.

In December 1817, when preparing his monumental painting of the signing of the Declaration of Independence, John Trumbull wrote Thomas Jefferson, the primary author of the Declaration, that Americans had a "universal interest" in "those Patriots to whom we owe that memorable Act and all its glorious consequences." Trumbull planned to have an engraving made of his painting so that Americans could see the forty-seven signers depicted in the painting. A portrait, however, no matter how accurate a rendition of the subject, provides only a limited perspective of a person. Word portraits are needed to flesh out the character of a person and equally important to provide descriptions of the relationships between individuals. William Plumer, an early U.S. senator from New Hampshire, believed that it was important to gather as many perspectives from as many people as possible to obtain an accurate description of a person. "A city appears very different when viewed from different positions—& so it is with a man. Viewed in different situations—different dispositions, the man thus examined appears unlike himself."

The great early national painter Charles Willson Peale wrote Thomas Jefferson telling him that a new pair of spectacles helped re-invigorate his interest in portraiture. Unfortunately, however, while wearing the glasses Peale usually painted his subject less than life size. Because such a diminution was unsatisfactory for Peale, he decided to paint the broad outlines and features of his subject without the aid of the spectacles and then fill in the detailed features later with the aid of the spectacles. So it is with word portraits. First we can obtain a broad picture of the individual by reading biographies and then deepen our understanding by gathering multiple quotations describing the individual.

Most of the quotations in this volume were taken from letters of the Founders. Other quotations appeared in journals, diaries, newspaper essays, and speeches. Some documentary editors choose to modernize their documents, while others provide literal transcriptions. I have accepted transcriptions as I found them. When drawing on original manuscripts, I have provided literal transcriptions. Editorial insertions within square brackets occur to obviate ambiguities in introducing quotations, to provide full names of individuals, and to avoid misunderstanding the archaic use of certain words, such as "nervous," meaning strong and powerful; "pathetic," meaning filled with emotion; and "want," meaning lacking.

I hope and expect that the Founders will come alive in these compilations and that we will get to know the Founding generation better than ever before, appreciating who the Founders were and what they did.

JPK
Madison, Wisconsin

Introduction

Born out of wedlock in 1755 on the British Caribbean island of Nevis, Alexander Hamilton's illegitimacy spurred him to excellence but also troubled him throughout his life. Once he achieved prominence, this humble—in Hamilton's eyes even humiliating—origin still threatened to undercut his achievements. His friends and political adherents admired his success; his opponents begrudged him. Hamilton always felt that his adversaries were ready and eager to denounce his origins and publicly humiliate him. He repeatedly felt compelled to prove to himself and to others—particularly political enemies—that he was worthy. As part of his political creed, he "desire[d] above all things to see the equality of political rights exclusive of all hereditary distinction firmly established."

In 1765 Hamilton's ne'er-do-well father abandoned the family. Ten-year-old Alexander and his mother moved to neighboring St. Croix, another West Indies island. With his mother's death three years later, Hamilton became a virtual orphan.

During these early years, Hamilton sensed that he was gifted. Soon others realized that he was bright and hardworking. Prominent men on the island befriended him—the Reverend Hugh Knox saw to his education and Nicholas Cruger hired him as a clerk in his trading house. Hamilton's ambition manifested early. At fifteen, he wrote to a friend of the "groveling" condition in which he was situated. Hamilton knew that his youth and social standing blocked any immediate significant advancement, but he vowed to "prepare the way for futurity." He was willing to risk his life, though not his character, for elevation in society. Perhaps, Hamilton pondered, a war might offer the chance to fulfill his ambition.

Hamilton's opportunity appeared in 1772 in the form of a devastating hurricane. The seventeen-year-old vividly described the storm's ferocity and the destruction it wreaked on life and property in a letter that was anonymously published. When Hamilton's authorship was revealed, his friends realized the young boy's potential. The islanders collected a fund to send Hamilton to the mainland to pursue his education, hoping that he would become a physician and return to St. Croix to establish a practice.

Hamilton arrived in New Jersey in 1772 and for a year attended a preparatory school. After being rejected by the College of New Jersey (Princeton), he applied to and was accepted at King's College (Columbia) in New York City. Though a devoted student, Hamilton got caught up in the Revolutionary controversy escalating between the American colonists and the imperial authorities in London. In 1774 he gave a stirring address to a public meeting and then wrote two pamphlets denouncing British policy. When fighting commenced in 1775, Hamilton helped to organize an artillery company and was commissioned a captain in the New York Line in 1776. In 1776 and 1777 he participated in several battles demonstrating both courage and leadership. In 1777, Commander-in-chief George Washington offered Hamilton a position in his military family as aide-de-camp with the rank of lieutenant colonel. The twenty-two-year-old eagerly accepted the invitation and soon became a trusted aide. Increasingly, Washington relied on Hamilton for advice and sent him on difficult and dangerous assignments. Hamilton's importance increased after the treaties with France in February 1778 because of his fluency in French.

Early during his military service, Hamilton had allied with

General George Clinton. But Clinton's departure from the army in July 1777, when he was elected New York's first governor, and Hamilton's 1780 marriage to Elizabeth Schuyler, the daughter of General Philip Schuyler (Clinton's erstwhile political opponent), realigned Hamilton politically. Abandoning the more democratic Clintonians, Hamilton became a strong advocate of the aristocratic Schuylerites.

After almost five years as Washington's aide, Hamilton chafed at the subservience that brought back memories of "groveling" in Cruger's store. Hamilton had hoped for a war; now he wanted to achieve glory on the battlefield. Using a disagreement with Washington as an excuse, Hamilton resigned his position and rejected Washington's apologetic overtures. At the same time, Hamilton brashly requested a field command from the commander he had just rebuffed. Magnanimously, Washington granted Hamilton's request, placing him as second in command in Lafayette's forces at the siege of Yorktown. There the two young officers successfully captured one of two fortified redoubts that led to the British surrender and soon the end of the war. Almost a decade later (thirty years after the youthful clerk had hoped for a war), Hamilton reflected on the opportunities provided by the Revolution.

> In those great revolutions which occasionally convulse society, human nature never fails to be brought forward in its brightest as well as in its blackest colors: And it has very properly been ranked not among the least of the advantages which compensate for the evils they produce, that they serve to bring to light talents and virtues which might otherwise have languished in obscurity or only shot forth a few scattered and wandering rays.
>
> *Hamilton: Eulogy on Nathanael Greene,*
> *New York, 4 July 1789*

After the victory at Yorktown, Hamilton retired from the army and moved to Albany where he studied law. Admitted to the New York bar in 1782, he moved to New York City after the British evacuation and established a successful law practice that found him defending former Loyalists in a variety of law suits. In 1782 and 1783 Hamilton served as a delegate to the Confederation Congress and wrote several essays, including "The Continentalist," a piece calling for a stronger central government. In 1785 Hamilton played an important role in establishing the Bank of New York, the first such financial institution in the state (and only the second in the entire country). Always opposed to slavery, Hamilton helped found New York's Society for Promoting the Manumission of Slaves in 1785.

In September 1786 Hamilton represented New York at the Annapolis Convention. The convention's commissioners hurriedly abandoned their apparent purpose: to propose commercial powers to strengthen the Confederation Congress. Instead the commissioners recommended a general convention of the states to meet in Philadelphia in May 1787 to consider broad changes to the Articles of Confederation—a proposal that Hamilton had made previously in 1780. While serving in the state assembly in 1787, Hamilton's fellow assemblymen elected him one of three delegates to represent New York in the upcoming Federal Convention in Philadelphia. Well known as a staunch supporter of strengthening Congress, the Assembly shackled Hamilton with Robert Yates and John Lansing, Jr., both from Albany and both averse to transferring state authority to Congress.

After listening to the radical Virginia Plan on 29 May 1787 and the moderate amendments suggested by small state delegates on 16 June, Hamilton on 18 June delivered a five-hour speech in which he outlined his ideas to create a powerful central government and all but eliminate the state governments. "The gentleman from New York is praised by every gentleman," Connecticut delegate William Samuel Johnson privately acknowledged, "but supported by no gentlemen." Continually out-voted by his fellow New York delegates, Hamilton left the Convention in early July and returned to New York City, from which he wrote to George Washington, who was serving as president of the Federal Convention, advocating that the Convention propose the best form of government that would then be vigorously defended and ratified. After Yates and Lansing left the Convention in mid-July, Hamilton returned to Philadelphia actively participating in the debate but unable to cast a vote for any measure. (The Convention's rules required at least two delegates to make an "official" delegation.) Despite his unofficial status, Hamilton signed the proposed Constitution for New York. The final Constitution was far weaker than he wanted, but Hamilton committed himself to work tirelessly for its ratification.

Hamilton's defense of the Constitution began two months before the Convention concluded. Seizing the initiative politically (as he had militarily during the war), Hamilton publicly denounced Governor Clinton as an opponent of the Convention. Hamilton would not allow the governor to stay above the fray, waiting for an advantageous moment to take a public stand. Although harshly criticized in the press for alienating the governor, Hamilton rightly anticipated Clinton's antifederalism and thus probably limited the governor's effectiveness in opposing the new Constitution.

New York Antifederalists wasted no time criticizing the newly proposed Constitution. "Cato," thought to be Governor Clinton, published the first of six newspaper essays beginning in late September 1787. Hamilton immediately responded with two essays signed by "Cæsar" in which New Yorkers were belligerently warned to accept the Constitution peacefully or have it forced upon them by an army led by the American

Fabius, a direct reference to George Washington. Sensing that his strong rhetoric had been counter-productive, Hamilton abandoned "Cæsar," opting instead for a more moderate voice. After a new Antifederalist started publishing essays under the pseudonym "Brutus," Hamilton and John Jay, the Confederation's secretary for foreign affairs, decided to write a systematic defense of the Constitution in a series of perhaps twenty essays. The introductory essay, written by Hamilton, appeared in the New York *Independent Journal* on 27 October 1787—a full six weeks after the Convention distributed the new Constitution. Jay wrote the next four essays. When Jay fell ill James Madison, a Virginia delegate attending Congress, joined the collaboration. Entitled "The Federalist," the series was written under the pseudonym "Publius" and appeared in several New York City newspapers. The eighty-five essays were also compiled in two volumes published in March and May 1788. Although the identity of "Publius" remained publicly undisclosed, Hamilton's authorship was widely presumed. Acknowledged as a superb analysis of the Constitution, "The Federalist" did little to assuage New York Antifederalists.

By the end of May 1788, eight states had already ratified the Constitution. Only one more was needed to implement the Constitution among the ratifying states. Virginia's state Convention had convened on 2 June, while New Hampshire's Convention that had met and recessed in February 1788 was scheduled to reconvene on 18 June. Observers expected that New Hampshire would ratify; Virginia's outcome was uncertain.

New York's ratifying Convention assembled in Poughkeepsie on 17 June 1788. Outnumbered by two-to-one, Federalist delegates faced a seemingly impossible challenge. Led by Hamilton and Jay, Federalists pursued a strategy of delay, hoping that news from New Hampshire and Virginia might force New York to join the Union. Hamilton attracted most of the attention and praise from observers of the Convention proceedings. In actuality, however, Jay was far more effective in appealing to pragmatic Antifederalist leaders, who agreed to ratify the Constitution after word arrived that both New Hampshire and Virginia had adopted.

Hamilton refused to stand for election to either the U.S. Senate or House of Representatives. He hoped, instead, to be appointed secretary of the treasury. President George Washington obliged and gained in Hamilton an able advisor. In a series of financial proposals that greatly favored the Northern States, and especially financial speculators, Hamilton rescued the near bankrupt country, but in the process divided the country politically. An opposition party was formed by Secretary of State Thomas Jefferson and his Virginia colleague James Madison. Madison had been allied with Hamilton in the Federal Convention and during the public debate over ratification, but now he opposed Hamilton's loose interpretation of the Constitution, his Northern-oriented economic proposals, and his preference for more friendly commercial relations with Great Britain. Washington agreed with Hamilton's proposals. Several attempts to discredit Hamilton failed.

In 1795 Hamilton resigned from public service and returned to his family and law practice in New York City. Though out of public office, Hamilton remained the acknowledged Federalist leader and habitually intrigued in national and state politics. In New York he opposed the re-election of Governor Clinton in 1792 and 1795 while supporting the candidacy of Chief Justice John Jay as Clinton's replacement.

At the national level, Hamilton continued to write pieces defending his economic policies, and he even drafted President Washington's "Farewell Address" that was published in newspapers in mid-September 1796. Many Federalists both in and out of office remained loyal to Hamilton—even members of Washington's and Adams' cabinets secretly looked to Hamilton as their leader. Despite his successes, Hamilton's illegitimacy occasionally resurfaced to haunt him. A poem in the Antifederalist *New York Journal* of 5 December 1787 began:

"From his own dunghill lately sprung,
So buxom, debonair, and young."

Even after his death, he was referred to on several occasions as "a bastard brat of a Scottish pedlar."

Both Adams and his wife, Abigail, came to despise Hamilton as a duplicitous intriguer who could never be appeased. The Adamses were right. In the 1796 presidential election, Hamilton sought to defeat Vice President Adams with Charles Cotesworth Pinckney, a prominent South Carolina lawyer, and a person susceptible to Hamilton's control. Hamilton strenuously opposed the election of Jefferson as president in 1796. In the election of 1800, Hamilton worked tirelessly behind the scenes against the re-election of President Adams, hoping that Thomas Pinckney, another South Carolina lawyer, would defeat the incumbent in the electoral vote. Hamilton denounced President Adams' public conduct and character in a scathing letter that circulated privately among Federalists. But when Jeffersonians inadvertently obtained a copy and published excerpts, Hamilton had the entire letter published as a pamphlet. The publication minimally contributed to Adams' defeat but caused many Federalists to question Hamilton's prudence. When Jefferson and Aaron Burr tied with the highest electoral vote, Hamilton lobbied with a religious fervor against Burr in the lame-duck Federalist House of Representatives, where the presidential election would be determined. Hamilton detested Jefferson, but he felt that Burr lacked a moral compass and would do anything for power and money. On the thirty-sixth roll-call vote, Jefferson finally received a majority of the state delegations' votes and was elected president. Hamilton won the enmity of Burr.

Burr's duplicity during the presidential election alienated him from the Jefferson administration, and Jefferson refused to have Burr as a running mate in the 1804 presidential election that was conducted under the provisions of the newly adopted Twelfth Amendment to the Constitution. In response, Burr shifted his focus to the New York gubernatorial election of 1804. Again, Hamilton energetically campaigned against Burr. Frustrated with this ardent opposition, Burr took advantage of an equivocal statement by Hamilton besmirching Burr and challenged Hamilton to a duel. Refusing to back down from the challenge, Hamilton left Manhattan, rowing up the Hudson River to meet Burr on the morning of 11 July 1804 at the heights of Weehawken, New Jersey—a traditional dueling ground on which Hamilton's eldest son had been killed just two years earlier. Hamilton, who would not fire his pistol, was mortally wounded by a single musket ball that pierced his liver and lodged in his spine. Thirty hours later he was dead.

Why would Hamilton risk so much in accepting Burr's challenge? Not only did he jeopardize his own life, but he also threatened the well-being of his large family and the political recovery and viability of the Federalist Party. What made him so foolhardy to expose himself and his country to such danger? Not all political figures of the time participated in the code duello—Washington, Jefferson, Adams, Madison, and John Jay neither challenged anyone to a duel nor did they accept challenges. Why was Hamilton unable to refuse Burr's challenge?

Hamilton's obscure origin, which had constantly haunted him, drove him to participate in the duel. He could not allow anyone the opportunity to question his courage and his honor. Honor was, in fact, the driving force in his life. He simply was psychologically unable to refuse Burr's challenge. Hamilton hoped that he would survive the duel and help the Federalist Party return to power, but he was unwilling to live with the shame that a refusal to duel might evoke. Thus, the obscurity that drove Hamilton's ambition to achieve greatness also mightily contributed to his premature death.

Not yet fifty years old at his death, Hamilton left a remarkable legacy. As Washington's nearest advisor during the war years and at the beginning of the national government under the new Constitution, Hamilton's policies helped to establish a solid economic foundation for the young country. He evoked admiration and loyalty among his followers and hatred and fear among his detractors. Though he was small in stature, even Hamilton's opponents viewed him intellectually as a Colossus. In his short life he successfully achieved the greatness that had seemed elusive in his earliest years. A man without a respectable past in the eyes of some of his contemporaries, Hamilton and his policies served as a harbinger of a new national future.

Hamilton hoped that the government he helped create would be a meritocracy in which upward mobility would be available to the deserving. He had defended the Constitution in a passage that certainly he saw as autobiographical.

> There are strong minds in every walk of life that will rise superior to the disadvantages of situation, and will command the tribute due to their merit, not only from the classes to which they particularly belong, but from the society in general. The door ought to be equally open to all; and I trust, for the credit of human nature, that we shall see examples of such vigorous plants flourishing in the soil of Fœderal, as well as of State Legislation.
>
> *Hamilton: The Federalist No. 36,*
> New York Packet, *8 January 1788*

Hamilton himself had accomplished his lofty goal—his vigorous plant had flourished in the new country he had done so much to erect.

Descriptions of
Alexander Hamilton

ALEXANDER HAMILTON TO EDWARD STEVENS, ST. CROIX,
11 NOVEMBER 1769
To confess my weakness, Ned, my Ambition is prevalent that I contemn the groveling and condition of a Clerk or the like, to which my Fortune &c. condemns me and would willingly risk my life though not my Character to exalt my Station. I'm confident, Ned, that my Youth excludes me from any hopes of immediate Preferment nor do I desire it, but I mean to prepare the way for futurity. I'm no Philosopher you see and may be justly said to Build Castles in the Air. My Folly makes me ashamed and beg you'll Conceal it, yet Neddy we have seen such Schemes successful when the Projector is Constant. I shall Conclude saying I wish there was a War.

ALEXANDER HAMILTON: *A FULL VINDICATION OF THE MEASURES OF CONGRESS,* NEW YORK, 15 DECEMBER 1774
I love to speak the truth. . . . 'Tis my maxim to let the plain naked truth speak for itself; and if men won't listen to it, 'tis their own fault; they must be contented to suffer for it.

ALEXANDER HAMILTON: "A SINCERE FRIEND TO AMERICA," *THE FARMER REFUTED &C.,* NEW YORK, 23 FEBRUARY 1775
I resume my pen, in reply [to Samuel Seabury's "Westchester Farmer"] . . . and can assure you that notwithstanding I am naturally of a grave and phlegmatic disposition, it has been the source of abundant merriment to me.

ALEXANDER HAMILTON TO JOHN JAY, MIDDLEBROOK, N.J.,
14 MARCH 1779
[AH endorses John Laurens' plan to raise two, three, or four black battalions] that I think their ~~stupidity~~ want of ~~knowledge~~ cultivation (for their natural faculties are ~~perhaps~~ probably as good as ours) joined to that habit of subordination which they

acquire from a life of servitude, will make them sooner become soldiers than our White inhabitants.

ALEXANDER HAMILTON TO JOHN LAURENS, MORRISTOWN, N.J., 8 JANUARY 1780
I am a stranger in this country. I have no property here, no connections. If I have talents and integrity (as you say I have), these are justly deemed very spurious titles in these enlightened days, when unsupported by others more solid.

ALEXANDER HAMILTON TO JOHN LAURENS, MORRISTOWN, N.J., 8 JANUARY 1780
I have strongly solicited leave to go to the Southward. It could not be refused; but arguments have been used to dissuade me from it, which however little weight they may have had in my judgment gave law to my feelings. I am chagrined and unhappy but I submit. In short Laurens I am disgusted with every thing in this world but yourself and *very* few more honest fellows and I have no other wish than as soon as possible to make a brilliant exit. 'Tis a weakness; but I feel I am not fit for this terrestrial Country.

ALEXANDER HAMILTON TO JOHN LAURENS, RAMAPO, N.J., 30 JUNE 1780
Have you not heard that I am on the point of becoming a benedict? I confess I am guilty. Next fall completes my doom. I give up my liberty to Miss Schuyler. She is a good hearted girl who I am sure will never play the termagant; though not a genius she has good sense enough to be agreeable, and though not a beauty, she has fine black eyes—is rather handsome and has every other requisite of the exterior to make a lover happy. And believe me, I am lover in earnest, though I

do not speak of the perfections of my Mistress in the enthusiasm of Chivalry.

ALEXANDER HAMILTON TO JOHN LAURENS,
NEW BRIDGE, N.J., 12 SEPTEMBER 1780
I hate Congress—I hate the army—I hate the world—I hate myself. The whole is a mass of fools and knaves.

MARQUIS DE LAFAYETTE TO GEORGE WASHINGTON,
PARAMUS, N.J., 28 NOVEMBER 1780
[On appointing an adjutant general for Washington's army] Unless, however you was to cast your Eye on a man who, I think, would suit better than any other in the world. Hamilton is, I confess, the officer whom I would like to see in that station. At equal advantages his services deserve from you the preference on any other. But his knowledge of Your opinions and intentions on Military arrangements, his love of discipline the advantages he would have on all the others principally when both armies will operate together, and his Uncommon Abilities would render him perfectly agreeable to you. The use of him would be increased by this preferment, and on other points he would render the same services. An Adjutant General ought always to be with the Commander in chief. Hamilton should therefore remain in your family, and his Great Industry for Business would render him perfectly serviceable in all circumstances. On every public or private account, My dear General, I would advise you to take him.

MARQUIS DE LAFAYETTE TO ALEXANDER HAMILTON,
PARAMUS, N.J., 28 NOVEMBER 1780
[Lafayette quoted and paraphrased his letter to Washington recommending Hamilton as his adjutant general.] I know the

general's friendship and gratitude for you, My Dear Hamilton, both are greater than you perhaps imagine. I am sure he needs only to be told that something will suit you and when he thinks he can do it he certainly will. Before this campaign I was your friend and very intimate friend, agreeable to the ideas of the World. Since my second voyage, my sentiment has increased to such a point, the world knows nothing about. To show *both* from want and from scorn of expressions I shall only tell you. Adieu

ALEXANDER HAMILTON TO JOHN LAURENS,
NEW WINDSOR, N.Y., 4 FEBRUARY 1781
A politician My Dear friend must be at all times supple—he must often dissemble.

GEORGE WASHINGTON TO JOHN SULLIVAN, NEW WINDSOR, 4 FEBRUARY 1781
How far Colo. Hamilton, of whom you ask my opinion as a financier, has turned his thoughts to that particular study I am unable to answer because I never entered upon a discussion on this point with him; but this I can venture to advance from a thorough knowledge of him, that there are few men to be found, of his age, who has a more general knowledge than he possesses, and none whose Soul is more firmly engaged in the cause, or who exceeds him in probity and Sterling virtue.

ALEXANDER HAMILTON TO JAMES MCHENRY,
NEW WINDSOR, N.Y., 18 FEBRUARY 1781
The Great man and I have come to an open rupture. Proposals of accommodation have been made on his part but rejected. I pledge my honor to you that he will find me inflexible. He shall for once at least repent his ill-humor. Without a shadow

of reason and on the slightest ground, he charged me in the most affrontive manner with treating him with disrespect. I answered very decisively—"Sir I am not conscious of it but since you have thought it necessary to tell me so, we part."

PHILIP SCHUYLER TO ALEXANDER HAMILTON,
ALBANY, N.Y., 25 FEBRUARY 1781

Long before I had the least Intimation that you intended that connection with my family, which is so very pleasing to me, and which affords me such entire satisfaction I had studied Your Character, and that of the other Gentlemen who composed the General's family. I thought I discovered in all an attention to the duties of their station, in some a considerable degree of ability, but (without a compliment for I trust there is no necessity of that between us), in you only I found those qualifications so essentially necessary to the man who is to aid and council a commanding General, environed with difficulties of every kind, and these perhaps more, and of greater magnitude, than any other ever has had to encounter, whose correspondence must of necessity be extensive always interesting, and frequently so delicate as to require much Judgment and address to be properly managed. The public voice has confirmed the Idea I had formed of You, but what is more consoling to me and more honorable to you, men of genius, Observation and Judgment think as I do on the occasion. Your quitting your station must therefore be productive of very material Injuries to the public, and this consideration, exclusive of others, impels me to wish that the unhappy breach should be closed, and a mutual Confidence restored. You may both of you Imagine when you separate, that the cause will remain a secret, but I will venture to speak decidedly, and say It is impossible, and I fear the Effect, especially with the French

Officers, with the French Minister, and even with the French Court; these already Observe so many divisions between us; they know and acknowledge your Abilities and how necessary you are to the General. Indeed how will the loss be replaced? He will if you leave him, have not one Gentleman left sufficiently versed in the French to convey his Ideas. And if he obtains one, it is more than probable that he will be a mere interpreter, without being able to afford his General an Idea, and Incapable of conducting business with any competent degree of address propriety or delicacy.

It is evident my Dear Sir that the General conceived himself the Aggressor, and that he quickly repented of the Insult; "he wished to heal a difference which could not have happened but in a moment of passion." It falls to the lot of few men to pass through life without one of those unguarded moments which wound the feelings of a friend; let us then impute them to the frailty of human nature, and with [Laurance] Sterne's recording angel, drop a tear, and blot It out of the page of life. I do not mean to reprehend the maxims you have formed for your conduct; they are laudable, and though generally approved, yet times and circumstances sometimes render a deviation necessary and Justifiable. This necessity now exists in the distresses of Your country. Make the sacrifice, the greater it is, the more glorious to you, your services are wanted, they are wanted in that particular station which You have already filled so beneficially to the public, and with such extensive reputation. I am as incapable of wishing as you are of doing, any thing injurious to those principles of honor, which If I may use the expression, are the test of virtue; my wishes, which are very earnest for a reconciliation I am convinced you will impute to their true motives, public good and the best affections of the human heart.

JOHN SULLIVAN TO GEORGE WASHINGTON, PHILADELPHIA,
6 MARCH 1781
I am happy to find your Excellency Entertains the Same Sentiments of the virtues and abilities of Colo. Hamilton, as I have Ever Done myself. After I wrote your Excellency I found The Eyes of Congress Turned on Robert Morris of this City as Financier. I did not therefore nominate Colo. Hamilton as I foresaw that it would be but a vain attempt. I Shall this Day nominate him as Secretary of Foreign Affairs on which I Think I Shall meet the Approbation of most of the States.

ALEXANDER HAMILTON TO ROBERT MORRIS,
DE PEYSTER'S POINT, N.Y., 30 APRIL 1781
I pretend not to be an able financier, it is a part of administration, which has been least in my way and of course has least occupied my inquiries and reflections. Neither have I had leisure or materials to make accurate calculations. I have been obliged to depend on memory for important facts for want of the authorities from which they are drawn. With all these disadvantages, my plan must necessarily be crude and defective; but if it may be a basis for something more perfect, or if it contains any hints that may be of use to you, the trouble I have taken myself, or may give you, will not be misapplied.

ALEXANDER HAMILTON TO ELIZABETH HAMILTON,
HEAD OF ELK, MD., 6 SEPTEMBER 1781
Every day confirms me in the intention of renouncing public life, and devoting myself wholly to you. Let others waste their time and their tranquillity in a vain pursuit of power and glory; be it my object to be happy in a quiet retreat with my better angel.

ALEXANDER HAMILTON TO THE MARQUIS DE LAFAYETTE,
ALBANY, N.Y., 3 NOVEMBER 1782

I have been employed for the last ten months in rocking the cradle and studying the art of fleecing my neighbors. I am now a Grave Counselor at law, and shall soon be a grand member of Congress. The Legislature at their last session took it into their heads to name me pretty unanimously one of their delegates. I am going to throw away a few months more in public life and then I retire a simple citizen and good paterfamilias. I set out for Philadelphia in a few days. You see the disposition I am in. You are condemned to run the race of ambition all your life. I am already tired of the career and dare to leave it.

ALEXANDER HAMILTON TO JOHN JAY, PHILADELPHIA,
25 JULY 1783

After having served in the field during the war, I have been making a short apprenticeship in Congress; but the evacuation of New York approaching, I am preparing to take leave of public life to enter into the practice of the law.

JAMES MCHENRY TO ALEXANDER HAMILTON,
PRINCETON, N.J., 22 OCTOBER 1783

The homilies you delivered in Congress are still recollected with pleasure. The impressions they made are in favor of your integrity and no one but believes you a man of honor and republican principles. Were you ten years older and twenty thousand pounds richer, there is no doubt but that you might obtain the suffrages of Congress for the highest office in their gift. You are supposed to possess various knowledge, useful—substantial—and ornamental. Your very grave and your cautious—your men who measure others by the standard of their own creeping politics think you sometimes intemperate, but seldom visionary, and that were you to pursue your object with as much cold perseverance as you do with ardor and argument you would become irresistible. In a word, if you could submit to spend a whole life in dissecting a fly you would be in their opinion one of the greatest men in the world.

HUGH KNOX TO ALEXANDER HAMILTON,
ST. CROIX, WEST INDIES, 28 JULY 1784

I have always had a just & secret pride in having Advised you to go to America, & in having recommended you to Some of my old friends there; Since you have not only Answered, but even far Exceeded, our most Sanguine hopes & Expectations. I am glad to find that your popularity increases, & that your fine talents are coming into play, in a way that Contributes so much to your own honor & Emolument, & to the Good of the public. Perhaps Camps & marches & the hardy deeds of War, may have a little fortified & Steeled your Constitution (which used to be rather delicate & frail). But beware you do not enfeeble & impair it again, by plunging into intense Studies, & the anxieties of the Bar: For I know your laudable Ambition to Excel, & that you will Strain Every Nerve to be among the first of your profession. And, great as your talent[s] are, I should imagine that the accurate Study of So Complex & Voluminous a Science as the law, & Acquiring all the habits of a pleader, would cost you a deal of Labor.

Your Matrimonial Connection, I should think, might Enable you to live at your ease (I do not mean the Otium inglorisum [inglorious leisure], but the otium honestum [honorable leisure]) As a Gentleman of Independent fortune, & to pursue Studies more pleasing to yourself & perhaps more profitable to the Commonwealth, & to posterity. You guess at the meaning of this hint. But you are certainly a better Judge of the propriety & Expediency of your present pursuits, than I can possibly be.

ALEXANDER HAMILTON TO ELIZABETH HAMILTON,
ANNAPOLIS, MD., 8 SEPTEMBER 1786

I wrote to you My beloved Betsey at Philadelphia; but through mistake brought off the letter with me; which I did not discover till my arrival here. I was not very well on the first part of the journey; but my health has been improved by travelling and is now as good as I could wish. Happy, however I cannot be, absent from you and my darling little ones. I feel that nothing can ever compensate for the loss of the enjoyments I leave at home, or can ever put my heart at tolerable ease. In the bosom of my family alone must my happiness be sought, and in that of my Betsey is every thing that is charming to me. Would to heaven I were there! Does not your heart re-echo the wish?

ALEXANDER HAMILTON: SPEECH IN THE NEW YORK
ASSEMBLY, 19 JANUARY 1787

I shall proceed under an impression that my constituents expect from me the free exercise of my judgment and the free declaration of my sentiments.

WILLIAM PIERCE: SKETCHES OF MEMBERS OF THE
CONSTITUTIONAL CONVENTION, 1787

Colo. Hamilton is deservedly celebrated for his talents. He is a practitioner of the Law, and reputed to be a finished Scholar. To a clear and strong judgment he unites the ornaments of fancy, and whilst he is able, convincing, and engaging in his eloquence the Heart and Head sympathize in approving him. Yet there is something too feeble in his voice to be equal to the strains of oratory;—it is my opinion that he is rather a convincing Speaker, than a blazing Orator. Colo. Hamilton requires time to think—he enquires into every part of his subject with the searchings of philosophy [i.e., science], and when he comes forward he comes highly charged with interesting matter, there is no skimming over the surface of a subject with him, he must sink to the bottom to see what foundation it rests on.—His language is not always equal, sometimes didactic like Bolingbroke's at others light and tripping like Stern's. His eloquence is not so defusive as to trifle with the senses, but he rambles just enough to strike and keep up the attention. He is about 33 years old, of small stature, and lean. His manners are tinctured with stiffness, and sometimes with a degree of vanity that is highly disagreeable.

ADRASTUS, NEW YORK JOURNAL, 6 SEPTEMBER 1787
[Warned readers to guard against] so dangerous a member of society, who, with a smooth tongue and double face, is capable of concealing and executing the worst intentions beneath the mask of sincerity and friendship.

INSPECTOR NO. 1, NEW YORK JOURNAL, 20 SEPTEMBER 1787
A man's knowledge is frequently over-rated in vulgar estimation in consequence of his having a memory good enough to retain a number of harmonious words which he can retail out at pleasure.—I know a negro who cannot read, and yet can deliver an extempore rhapsody, that will captivate weak minds, and give not offence, even to the ears of intelligent men.

I have also known an upstart attorney, palm himself upon a great and good man [i.e., George Washington], for a youth of extraordinary genius, and under the shadow of such a patronage make himself at once known and respected; but being sifted and bolted to the brann, he was, at length, found to be a superficial, self-concerted coxcomb, and was of course turned off, and disregarded by his patron.

I have known a blockhead publish pamphlets with borrowed phrases and arguments, by which he acquired a reputation he never was entitled to.

I have also known a man publish pieces of his own composition, which, on examination, I have found to be mere froth, calculated only to bewilder the understanding.

NEW YORK JOURNAL, 5 DECEMBER 1787
What in nature, observes a correspondent, is more despicable than a FOP,———The Fop, says a modern poet, most resembles the gay mushroom;—as,

> From his own dunghill lately sprung,
> So buxom, debonair, and young;
> Yet on his brow sits empty scorn,—
> "He hates mechanics, meanly born."
> Stranger to merit—genius—sense—
> He owes his rise to impudence,
> With strutting self-importance fraught,
> Free—from each particle of thought;
> He'll not debase himself to think,—
> "'Tis too damn'd low,"—but he will drink.
> From his own lips his praises flow,
> With—"Damme! I did so and so!—
> I've e'en in paths of honor trod;
> I'd soon, go to hell!—by God!—
> Than lose my honor!"—yet his genius
> Consists in blasphemy and meanness;
> In what true honor interdicts,
> And in diverting little tricks.
> He'll, all at once, start from his chair,
> Twirl his whip and sing an air,
> Dance, to show his grace and shape,
> Brisk and sprightly as an—Ape.
> To the glass he often goes,
> There adjusts his stock and clothes,

Meets his image with a glance,
Of the sweetest complaisance.
He's first,—and oft the only one,—
To laugh at his own jest or pun.
Suppose it is wond'rous witty,
But men of sense will—smile and pity.
Such is the hero of my poem,
Readers—you must surely know him.

ALEXANDER HAMILTON TO ANGELICA SCHUYLER CHURCH,
NEW YORK, 6 DECEMBER 1787
I seldom write to a lady without fancying the relation of lover and mistress. It has a very inspiring effect. And in your case the dullest materials could not help feeling that propensity.

JAMES KENT TO NATHANIEL LAWRENCE,
POUGHKEEPSIE, N.Y., 21 DECEMBER 1787
You may praise who you please & I will presume to say that I think Publius is a most admirable writer & wields the sword of Party dispute with justness, energy, & inconceivable dexterity. The Author *must be* Hamilton who I think in Genius & political Research is not inferior to Gibbon, Hume or Montesquieu.

HUGH HUGHES, "INTERROGATOR" TO PUBLIUS OR THE
PSEUDO-FEDERALIST, DECEMBER 1787*
You appear to be much bloated by a vain Opinion of a little Learning and Knowledge, and not infrequently to have written like a Person, who considered himself as the sole Proprietor of all common Sense, permit me to remind you of the Fable of the Ox and the Frog, who, ambitious to make as great an Appearance as the Former, kept straining its lanky Sides till it

burst, which, must be the Fate of every Individual whatever, that attempts to put his scanty Knowledge or Acquirements in Competition with the Aggregate Knowledge of a Nation— Only reflect on how little you know of your own mental and corporal Composition, as well as of what daily and momently contributes to your Support and Existence or, that many of the most simple Plebeians, or Mechanics, can teach you some of the first Principles of Philosophy. Or how very little you know of any Thing, when compared with what is unknown to you and Thousands who are much wiser, & you will not find much Cause to value yourself an Omniscience.

*Taken from an unpublished manuscript in the Library of Congress.

SAMUEL BLACHLEY WEBB TO JOSEPH BARRELL, NEW YORK, 13 JANUARY 1788

We have in the Press a Pamphlet written by Colonel Hamilton under the Signature of Publius on the subject of a Federal Government, which I will send you by the first conveyance. He is undoubtedly one of the most sensible men in America, though yet not much more than Thirty years old.

COLLIN MCGREGOR TO NEIL JAMIESON, NEW YORK, 18 FEBRUARY 1788

I do most heartily approve of your writing a Complimentary letter to Colo. Hamilton. He is a worthy Character and has Considerable Interest in this State, which I am clear will every day increase. His unshaken integrity & Conspicuous Abilities will soon place him at the head of Affairs, and as you have so much property in this State, keeping or renewing friendship with a person of this distinction I think is of much Consequence to your Interest.

Descriptions of Alexander Hamilton

A CITIZEN, AND REAL FRIEND TO ORDER AND GOOD
GOVERNMENT, NEW YORK *DAILY ADVERTISER*,
21 MARCH 1788

The publications of Col. Hamilton, in defense of the liberties of America previous to the late war, when a youth in the college of New York; his great military services, and the confidential line in which he stood with that good and great man General Washington, during that war, are indubitable proofs of his virtue. As a lawyer, a politician, and a statesman, Col. Hamilton is certainly great; as a public speaker he is clear, pointed and sententious; he excels most men in reply, being possessed of the powers of reasoning in an eminent degree, and he is endowed with a most benevolent and good heart.

DAVID S. BOGART TO SAMUEL BLACHLEY WEBB,
POUGHKEEPSIE, N.Y., 14 JUNE 1788
... Mr. Hamilton, the American Cicero. ...

CHARLES TILLINGHAST TO JOHN LAMB, POUGHKEEPSIE,
N.Y., 21 JUNE 1788
You would be surprised, did you not know the Man, what an amazing Republican Hamilton wishes to make himself to be considered—*But he is known*—

PHILIP SCHUYLER TO JOHN BRADSTREET SCHUYLER,
POUGHKEEPSIE, N.Y., 26 JUNE 1788
Though all [the Federalist speakers in the New York Convention] are eloquent, Hamilton and his sentiments are so true, his judgment so correct, his elocution so pleasing, so smooth, and yet so forcible that he reaches the heart and carries conviction, where every avenue to conviction is shut up. I fear there are too many, who labor under this prejudice.

SAMUEL BLACHLEY WEBB TO CATHERINE HOGEBOOM,
POUGHKEEPSIE, N.Y., 27 JUNE 1788
We have been entertained for upwards of two hours this morning by Colonel Hamilton in one of the most elegant speeches I ever heard. He is indeed one of the most remarkable genius's of the Age, his Political knowledge exceeds, I believe, any Man in our Country, and his Oratorial abilities has pleased his friends and surprised his Enemies.

GEORGE CLINTON TO JOHN LAMB, POUGHKEEPSIE, N.Y.,
28 JUNE 1788
I steal this Moment while the Convention is in Committee and the little Great Man employed in repeating over Parts of Publius to us, to drop you a Line.

ALEXANDER HAMILTON: SPEECH IN THE NEW YORK
RATIFYING CONVENTION, 28 JUNE 1788
I am apprehensive that in the warmth of my feelings, I may have uttered expressions, which were too vehement. If such has been my language, it was from the habit of using strong phrases to express my ideas.

ROBERT C. JOHNSON TO WILLIAM SAMUEL JOHNSON,
POUGHKEEPSIE, N.Y., 28 JUNE 1788
I am this moment returned [from the state ratifying Convention] from hearing Hamilton—warm, animated, clear, logical & convincing; attracting, nay, forcing universal admiration & applause. And he is at present an Enthusiast—... I have heard Hamilton with rapture & admiration.

MELANCTON SMITH TO NATHAN DANE,
POUGHKEEPSIE, N.Y., 28 JUNE 1788
Hamilton is the champion, he speaks frequently, very long and

very vehemently—has, like Publius, much to say not very applicable to the subject—

POUGHKEEPSIE *COUNTRY JOURNAL*, 1 JULY 1788
[Commenting on the New York ratifying Convention.] The spectators who seldom make a number less than a hundred and oftentimes are twice so many, enjoy a mental feast exquisite as uncommon. The first geniuses of the country have here a field on which their powers have ample room. Under the federal banner Col. H—— stands the political porcupine, armed at all points, and brandishes a shaft to every opposer: A shaft, powerful to repel, and keen to wound.

ALEXANDER HAMILTON: SPEECH IN THE NEW YORK RATIFYING CONVENTION, 11 JULY 1788
It has been industriously circulated that I am a man of such Talents as to carry any Cause.

NEW YORK *DAILY ADVERTISER*, 16 JULY 1788
He [John Jay] was soon followed by Mr. Hamilton, who in a most argumentative and impassioned address, demonstrated that the proposition before the Committee, would be a total rejection of the Constitution. He opened with a beautiful exordium, in which he described in a delicate but most affecting manner the various ungenerous attempts to prejudice the minds of the Convention against him. He had been represented as an ambitious man, a man unattached to the interests and insensible to the feelings of the people; and even his supposed talents had been wrested to his dishonor, and produced as a charge against his integrity and virtue. He called on the world to point out an instance in which he had ever deviated from the line of public or private duty. The pathetic [i.e., moving]

appeal fixed the silent sympathetic gaze of the spectators, and made them all his own.

NEW YORK *DAILY ADVERTISER,* 21 JULY 1788
The next day (Thursday), previous to taking the question on this motion, Mr. Hamilton made another display of those great abilities for which he is justly distinguished; he was powerful in his reasoning, and so persuasively eloquent and pathetic [i.e., emotional], that he drew tears from most of the audience.

RICHARD PLATT TO WINTHROP SARGENT, NEW YORK, 8 AUGUST 1788
Little Hamilton shines like a Star of the first magnitude. Think how great his Victory in our Convention when with only 19 Federalists opposed to 46 most violent Anti's with Clinton, Yates, Lansing, Smith & Jones at their head, after six or seven weeks, he triumphed & gave us the Constitution.

JAMES KENT: MEMOIRS
Colonel Hamilton was indisputably pre-eminent [at the bar]. This was universally conceded. He rose at once to the loftiest heights of professional eminence by his profound penetration, his power of analysis, the comprehensive grasp and strength of his understanding, and the firmness, frankness, and integrity of his character.

He generally spoke with much animation and energy and with considerable gesture. His language was clear, nervous [i.e., strong, powerful], and classical. His investigations penetrated to the foundation and reason of every doctrine and principle which he examined, and he brought to the debate a mind filled with all the learning and precedents applicable to the subject. He never omitted to meet, examine, and discover the strength or weakness, the truth or falsehood of every proposition with which he had to contend. His candor was magnanimous and rose to a level with his abilities. His temper was spirited but courteous, amiable and generous, and he frequently made pathetic [i.e., emotional] and powerful appeals to the moral sense and patriotism, the fears and hopes of the assembly, in order to give them a deep sense of the difficulties of the crisis and prepare their minds for the reception of the Constitution.

BRISSOT DE WARVILLE: *NEW TRAVELS IN THE UNITED STATES OF AMERICA,* AUGUST 1788

Mr. Hamilton is Mr. Madison's worthy rival as well as his collaborator. He looks thirty-eight or forty years old, is not tall, and has a resolute, frank, soldierly appearance. He was aide-de-camp to General Washington, who had the greatest confidence in him, a confidence he deserved. Since the war he has resumed the practice of law and has devoted himself mainly to public life. Elected to Congress, he has distinguished himself by his eloquence and by the soundness of his reasoning. Among the works which have come from his pen the most distinguished are a large number of letters inserted in *The Federalist,* of which I shall speak hereafter, and the *Letters from Phocion,* published in defense of the Loyalists. During the war Mr. Hamilton fought the Loyalists with success, but when peace came it was his opinion that they should not be driven to desperation by harsh persecution, and he was fortunate enough to win over to clemency his fellow citizens, who had been inspired by a justifiable resentment against the Loyalists because of the damage they had done. This young orator's moment of triumph came at the New York Convention. The Antifederalist party was strong in New York City,* and three-quarters of the members of the convention when they left for

Poughkeepsie were opposed to the new Constitution. Mr. Hamilton, joining his efforts to those of the celebrated Mr. Jay, succeeded in convincing even the most obstinate among them that the refusal of New York would have disastrous consequences for the state and for the Confederation. Consequently they voted in favor of the Constitution. The celebration in New York following the ratification was magnificent. The ship *Federalist,* which took part in the festivities, was renamed *Hamilton* in honor of this eloquent orator.

Hamilton married General Schuyler's daughter, a delightful woman who combines both the charms and attractions and the candor and simplicity typical of American womanhood. . . . Mr. Hamilton had the determined appearance of a republican.

*Antifederalists were very weak in New York City, but did control two-thirds of the New York Convention at its outset.

EDMUND RANDOLPH TO JAMES MADISON, RICHMOND, VA., 3 SEPTEMBER 1788

I reverence Hamilton, because he was honest and open in his views.

LOUIS-GUILLAUME OTTO: BIOGRAPHIES OF AMERICAN STATESMEN, FALL 1788

Great orator, intrepid in public debates. Zealous partisan, to an extreme over the new Constitution, and declared enemy of Governor Clinton, whom he had the courage to attack publicly in a newspaper without any provocation. He is one of those rare men who have distinguished themselves equally on the field of battle and at the bar. He owes everything to his talents. An indiscretion got him into trouble with General Washington for whom he served as confidential secretary; other indiscretions obliged him to leave Congress in 1783. He has a little too much pretension and too little prudence.

Here is what M. Luzerne said about him in 1780: "Mr. Hamilton, one of the aides de camp of General Washington who has the most influence with him, man of spirit, of a mediocre integrity; he left the English territory where he was born of low extraction . . . Also a favorite of M. de Lafayette. Mr. [Thomas] Conway thinks that Hamilton hates the French, that he is absolutely corrupted and that the connections that he will appear to have with us will never be anything but deceptive."

Mr. Hamilton has done nothing that could justify this last opinion; he is only too impetuous and because he wants to control everything, he fails in his intentions. His eloquence is often out of place in public debates, where precision and clarity are preferred to a brilliant imagination. It is believed that Mr. Hamilton is the author of the pamphlet entitled *The Federalist*. He has again missed his mark. This work is of no use to educated men and it is too learned and too long for the ignorant. It has, however, made him a great celebrity and a small frigate has been named *Hamilton* which was pulled through the streets of New York during the great federal procession. But these parades only make a momentary impression here and as the Antifederalist party is the largest in the state, Mr. Hamilton has lost more than he has gained by his zeal on this occasion.

An immigrant in this state, where he rose by benevolence, Mr. Hamilton has found the means to run off with the daughter of General Schuyler,* a great proprietor and very influential. After being reconciled with the family, he now possesses the esteem of his father-in-law.

*Otto: Elopement is more common in America than in France; the parents are offended at first, they wait and are reconciled after a few months. Everyone is interested in these passionate marriages, since they seem to conform to the primitive natural impulses.

THOMAS LEE SHIPPEN TO THOMAS JEFFERSON, LONDON,
3 FEBRUARY 1789

Mr. S. Morris son of General Morris of New York is just arrived from America. He gives me a very interesting account of the proceedings of the New York Convention in which Hamilton makes a godlike figure indeed.

ABRAHAM CLARK TO JONATHAN DAYTON, MARCH 1789

I feel myself out of all patience with Col. Hamilton. He really appears to be, what I have some times thought him, a shim sham politician. He must needs soon run himself aground. His politics are such as will not stand the test. He will soon refine them to nothing.

A SPECTATOR, *NEW YORK PACKET*, 3 MARCH 1789

It would be a difficult task . . . to attempt doing justice to the clear argumentative and finished powers of Col. Hamilton. Suffice it to observe, that [Hamilton] challenged the confidence of every spectator, and gained it.

TRISTRAM LOWTHER TO JAMES IREDELL, NEW YORK,
9 MAY 1789

The popularity of Col. Hamilton has been hurt by his declining to represent this district in Congress; it is supposed he looks up to be Financier-General, for which he has been preparing himself, or to be appointed a foreign ambassador, for either of which he is extremely well qualified. He is said and believed to be a man of such extraordinary powers as to be able to render himself master of any subject in a week.

LETTER FROM NEW YORK, PHILADELPHIA *INDEPENDENT GAZETTEER*, 9 JUNE 1789

[In talking about Hamilton as the third of three candidates who might be named Secretary of the Treasury] The third is certainly a man of considerable talents for his years and experience; but it is thought that his present qualifications are better adapted to the law department than that of the treasury. He has obtained a high degree of popularity in this city, and if he has skill to manage it properly, his consequence must increase. But when the pulse of party beats so high as it has lately done, the tide of popularity is liable to great change. At present the people of this city think no office too high for him, and hence he is the most talked of among us for the head of the treasury.

WILLIAM SMITH (OF MARYLAND) TO OTHO H. WILLIAMS, NEW YORK, 7 JULY 1789
Colo. Hamilton is Spoke of here to fill the Secretary's office to the treasury. He delivered a very elegant Panegyrick on Saturday last by order of the Cincinnati, to the memory of Genl. Greene in which he took occasion to compliment very highly some of the officers who were engaged in the Southern war Particularly [John Eager] Howard, & Colo. [William] Washington, but as his Eulogium did not extend to all who were active there, tis said he has offended many. I expect the Oration will be printed, if so I will Send it to Baltimore. I thought the composition elegant, & a good Narrative of Genl. Greene's conduct throughout the war but especially to the Southward, was pretty well delivered to a very crowded audience, although Hamilton is by no means a good Speaker or orator. What his talents may be as a financier I know not.

FISHER AMES TO JOHN LOWELL, NEW YORK, 13 SEPTEMBER 1789
I think so highly of Col. Hamilton's moral & intellectual qualities that I consider his appointment to the head of the Treasury as an auspicious event.

COMTE DE MOUSTIER TO COMTE DE MONTMORIN,
NEW YORK, 17 SEPTEMBER 1789

I have no doubt that Mr. Hamilton genuinely wishes to fulfill the responsibilities of the United States toward His Majesty. He was born English and I do not believe him very well disposed toward France; he would like nothing better than to put it in closer relations with the Estates General of the Low Countries, current Allies of England. . . . to judge him by his association with well-known and brazen speculators and stockjobbers.

OLIVER WOLCOTT, JR., TO ELIZABETH WOLCOTT,
NEW YORK, 24 SEPTEMBER 1789

From the appearance of Col. Hamilton, I think him a very amiable, plain man, and one whom I expect to like on acquaintance.

JAMES MCHENRY TO ALEXANDER HAMILTON,
BALTIMORE, MD., 7 OCTOBER 1789

Be assured I was not only made exceedingly happy by your appointment but shall always rejoice at every circumstance which can add either to your fame or fortune. Your office is vastly important, and you are worthy of it, and what is more, equal to its duties, but at the same time it is extremely hazardous. I cannot tell whether all the wisdom and justice and policy and politics you can put into your plans will procure them in all conjunctures a good reception in Congress; or rather, for how many ages these qualities will serve instead of the means which a British minister employs to ensure success to his.

JOHN FENNO TO JOSEPH WARD, 10 OCTOBER 1789

Great things are anticipated from Hamilton. I think that he considers his fame as much at stake as ever a General of an

Army did—and I think further, that he is one of those sort of men that consider wealth as less than nothing and vanity contrasted with Honor & reputation—These things being so—it appears to me that now is the time for a stroke—but your penetrating eye may see dangers in Ambush which escape me.

JOHN TRUMBULL TO OLIVER WOLCOTT, JR.,
HARTFORD, CONN., 9 DECEMBER 1789
I almost envy you the friendship of Col. Hamilton, with whom I doubt not, you are in the closest habits of intimacy. However, till I have the honor of a personal acquaintance with him, I will not depose on oath that he is half so great or good a man as I think him.

ANGELICA SCHUYLER CHURCH TO ALEXANDER HAMILTON,
LONDON, 4 FEBRUARY 1790
My father's [Philip Schuyler] letters have relieved me from the *dread* of having offended him. He speaks of you with so much pride and satisfaction, that if I did not love you as he does, I should be a little Jealous of his attachment.

OLIVER WOLCOTT, SR., TO OLIVER WOLCOTT, JR.,
LITCHFIELD, CONN., 8 FEBRUARY 1790
The gentleman at the head of the department, with whom I am most acquainted, I have always known to be a man of strict integrity and honor.

SAMUEL JOHNSTON TO JAMES IREDELL, 25 FEBRUARY 1790
The great difficulty seems to rest on the ways and means; but your favorite, the Secretary of the Treasury, whose application is as indefatigable as his genius is extensive, encourages us to hope that they may be found.

THOMAS HARTLEY TO JASPER YEATES, NEW YORK,
4 APRIL 1790
He is a man of Spirit.

JOHN TRUMBULL TO JOHN ADAMS, HARTFORD, CONN.,
17 APRIL 1790
By the way is our Secretary H. a great Politician, or only a theoretical genius—He has great abilities [to] be sure—but I doubt his knowledge of mankind—I have never spoken my sentiments on his report [on public credit]—but I really fear some parts of his plan are too complicated—& perhaps at this period impolitic as well as impracticable.

JOHN ADAMS TO JOHN TRUMBULL, NEW YORK,
25 APRIL 1790
Our Secretary [of the Treasury] has however I think good Abilities and certainly great Industry. He has high minded Ambition and great Penetration.—He may have too much disposition to intrigue.—If this is not indulged I know not where a better Minister for his Department could be found. But nothing is more dangerous, nothing will be more certainly destructive in our Situation than the Spirit of Intrigue.

　　I thank you kindly for your anecdote about throwing away votes. Both H—n and W—b [Hamilton and Samuel Blachley Webb] were for me, and I really suspect that they had some real fears that I might have the greatest number of votes, yet in all supposition it was a corrupt intrigue and an insidious maneuver.

WILLIAM MACLAY: JOURNAL, PHILADELPHIA, 28 JUNE 1790
Hamilton has a very boyish giddy Manner. Our Scotch Irish People would call him a Skite.

ALEXANDER HAMILTON TO WALTER STEWART, NEW YORK,
5 AUGUST 1790
I like elbow room in a yard.

JOHN WHEELOCK TO ALEXANDER HAMILTON,
DARTMOUTH COLLEGE, N.H., 27 AUGUST 1790
The Trustees of this literary Institution have desired me to express their congratulations at the prosperous state of our national finances under your wise direction. They have desired me to communicate the high sense, which they retain of your talents, and political knowledge.

Influenced by an exalted Opinion of your merit, they make a tender of the highest Honors, that any University can confer. They beg, Sir, your acceptance of the *Degree* of *Doctor* of the *Laws* of *Nature* and *Nations*. It is a testimony unequal to their respect; but it is the best within their power to give. The Diploma will be completed, and forwarded to you by some safe conveyance, so soon as may be convenient.

LOUIS GUILLAUME OTTO TO COMTE DE MONTMORIN,
PHILADELPHIA, 24 DECEMBER 1790
At no time has Mr. Hamilton's reputation been so well established as since the publication of the report, which has been avidly read by all classes of citizens.

WILLIAM CHANNING TO THEODORE FOSTER,
NEWPORT, R.I., 8 JANUARY 1791
Mr. Hamiltons Character stands high with us—He merits much from his Country May he be long Victorious in the arduous conflict in which he is engaged It is a painful reflection that A Man of his Virtues & abilities must finally be vanquish'd—

JAMES SULLIVAN TO JOHN LANGDON, BOSTON,
8 JANUARY 1791
I conceive that the General Government has been hitherto managed in a most Masterly manner. the department of the treasury has mostly attracted the notice of the people, as well from its having been the most interesting part of the Government as from its being most operative. the Secretary of the Treasury Exhibits great ability as well as great assiduity in his business, and proves himself quite fitted for the important office assigned him. Should he prove unsuccessfull in some of his plans it would not alter my opinion of him and tho' I do not agree to all his measures yet I have still the opinion of him which I have expressed.

THOMAS RUSSELL TO JOHN LANGDON, BOSTON,
10 JANUARY 1791
Every publication I see of the Secretary of the Treasury—does him honour—and proves the wisdom of the Choice, of so Excellant a Man, for that important Appointment.

HENRY VAN SCHAACK TO THEODORE SEDGWICK,
PITTSFIELD, MASS., 10 JANUARY 1791
The Secretary seems in all his Reports to possess talents to Investigate matters referred to him with equal ability and industry—and I do most sincerely hope to see his labours adopted in the whole. If we do not Manifast a great degree of faith in this great Man I fear our systems of Finance will come forward in a crippled condition. I am sorry to see so many of your people fond of tackling frequently about matters that are nearly as far above their understandings as they are beyond mine.

Descriptions of Alexander Hamilton

LETTER FROM BOSTON, GAZETTE OF THE UNITED STATES, 19 JANUARY 1791

The Secretary's Report of the plan of a National Bank appears to be calculated for good national purposes, and, if adopted, will completely establish the credit of the United States. I think Hamilton will rise to fame as a Financier. He has a fine field, and if Congress support him, as I think they will, (policy and experience being incontestibly in favor of the idea, and I may justly add, the public opinion too,) he will become a star of the first magnitude in our political hemisphere, and a luminary to the world.

JOHN ADAMS TO JOHN TRUMBULL, PHILADELPHIA, 23 JANUARY 1791

The Secretary of the Treasury is all that you think him. There is no office in the Government better filled.

HENRY VAN SCHAACK TO THEODORE SEDGWICK, BENNINGTON, VT., 25 JANUARY 1791

I wish I had it in my power to impeach all the members of your house on the ground of an intention to distroy the Secy. of the Treasury—The people among us and here find great fault with Congress to refer so many paltry matters to this truly great & valuable man, whose labors say they ought to be confined to the great and weighty objects of Government. He is considered as a jewel of great estimation in bringing our glorious Government to perfection. The loss of such a man wod. derange and Embarrass the Government exceedingly—Why will not Congress commit the trivial matter of a petition for a little compensation to a Committee? all References, the small ones I mean, are considered as resulting from Indolence in some of your Members. If the Secy. has time to receive the most respectful compliments from a man of my obscurity pray make them in a way you know how.

JOSEPH STANTON AND THEODORE FOSTER TO GOVERNOR ARTHUR FENNER, PHILADELPHIA, 17 FEBRUARY 1791

The Confidence of the Nation at large in the Secretary of the Treasury is deservedly great. Possessed of a contemplative, comprehensive, energetic, independent Mind, he Unites the strictest Integrity to the most indefatigable Industry, which on all occasions he incessantly applies to the Service of the Public. Prudent, active yet deliberate, Studious, firm and candid he may be said to invigorate the whole fiscal System of our Country. Ability, Foresight, Decision and a comprehensive View of the remotest Consequences, are so conspicuous in all his Reports respecting the Finances and National Arrangements which he recommends that they seem generally to carry conviction as they go. With a Fertile Invention, added to real Science and Patriotic Views, he has the Talent of bringing his Information into Action, with that Perspicuity, Method & Forcibleness of Reasoning that his Country Generally acquiesces in the Propriety of the Measures he recommends.

ROBERT TROUP TO ALEXANDER HAMILTON, NEW YORK, 15 JUNE 1791

There was every appearance of a passionate courtship between the Chancellor [Robert R. Livingston], Burr, Jefferson & Madison when the two latter were in Town. Delenda est Carthago [Carthage must be destroyed] I suppose is the Maxim adopted with respect to you. They had better be quiet, for if they succeed they will tumble the fabric of the government in ruins to the ground. Upon this subject however I cannot say that I have the smallest uneasiness. You are too well seated in the hearts of the citizens of the Northern & Middle States to be hunted down by them. That your foes may be confounded & that your administration may increase in success & luster is the cordial wish of. . . .

NATHANIEL HAZARD TO ALEXANDER HAMILTON,
NEW YORK, 25 NOVEMBER 1791

I enclose for your Amusement, Trumbull's last letter to me. He communes with very few intensely. He is a Man of a very independent Spirit. He is avowedly the Friend of C____H_____n [Colonel Hamilton]. Doctor [William Samuel] Johnson is so likewise, as you shall presently judge. The Doctor spoke humbly of J_____n [Jefferson] at [Pierpont] Edwards' Table. At his Lodgings, I asked him what he thought of M_____n [Madison], as compared with H_____n [Hamilton], "He (M_____n) ought not to be mentioned in the same Day with H_____n."

ALEXANDER HAMILTON TO EDWARD CARRINGTON,
PHILADELPHIA, 26 MAY 1792

As to my own political Creed, I give it to you with the utmost sincerity. I am affectionately attached to the Republican theory. I desire *above all things* to see the *equality* of political rights exclusive of all hereditary distinction firmly established by a practical demonstration of its being consistent with the order and happiness of society.

As to State Governments, the prevailing bias of my judgment is that if they can be circumscribed within bounds consistent with the preservation of the National Government they will prove useful and salutary. If the States were all of the size of Connecticut, Maryland or New Jersey, I should decidedly regard the local Governments as both safe & useful. As the thing now is, however, I acknowledge the most serious apprehensions that the Government of the United States will not be able to maintain itself against their influence. I see that influence already penetrating into the National Councils & perverting their direction.

Hence a disposition on my part towards a liberal construction of the powers of the National Government and to erect every fence to guard it from depredations, which is, in my opinion, consistent with constitutional propriety.

As to any combination to prostrate the State Governments I disavow and deny it. From an apprehension lest the Judiciary should not work efficiently or harmoniously I have been desirous of seeing some rational scheme of connection adopted as an amendment to the Constitution, otherwise I am for maintaining things as they are, though I doubt much the possibility of it, from a tendency in the nature of things towards the preponderancy of the State Governments.

I said, that I was affectionately attached to the Republican theory. This is the real language of my heart which I open to you in the sincerity of friendship; & I add that I have strong hopes of the success of that theory; but in candor I ought also to add that I am far from being without doubts. I consider its success as yet a problem.

It is yet to be determined by experience whether it be consistent with that stability and order in Government which are essential to public strength & private security and happiness. On the whole, the only enemy which Republicanism has to fear in this Country is in the Spirit of faction and anarchy. If this will not permit the ends of Government to be attained under it—if it engenders disorders in the community, all regular & orderly minds will wish for a change—and the demagogues who have produced the disorder will make it for their own aggrandizement. This is the old Story.

If I were disposed to promote Monarchy & overthrow State Governments, I would mount the hobby horse of popularity—

I would cry out usurpation—danger to liberty &c. &c.—I would endeavor to prostrate the National Government—raise a ferment—and then "ride in the Whirlwind and direct the Storm."* That there are men acting with Jefferson & Madison who have this in view I verily believe. I could lay my finger on some of them. That Madison does *not* mean it I also verily believe, and I rather believe the same of Jefferson; but I read him upon the whole thus—"A man of profound ambition & violent passions."

*Originally in Joseph Addison's *The Campaign* (1704), but then repeated in Alexander Pope's third book of *The Dunciad* (1729).

ALEXANDER HAMILTON TO PRESIDENT GEORGE
WASHINGTON, PHILADELPHIA, 18 AUGUST 1792
I trust that I shall always be able to bear, as I ought, imputations of error of judgment; but I acknowledge that I cannot be entirely patient under charges which impeach the integrity of my public motives or conduct.

ALEXANDER HAMILTON TO SUSANNA LIVINGSTON,
PHILADELPHIA, 29 DECEMBER 1792
Of all delinquencies, those towards the Ladies I think the most inexcusable. And hold myself bound by all the laws of chivalry to make the most ample reparation in any mode you shall prescribe. You will of course recollect that I am a married man!

JOHN BARD TO ALEXANDER HAMILTON, NEW YORK,
4 MARCH 1793
I dined a few days ago with a large Company at Judge [William] Duane's. In the course of the after noon, you became the Subject of general Conversation. It gave me the greatest pleasure to hear that Just and grateful applause which all the

Company bestowed upon you. Your Friend General [Horatio] Gates declared when ever your Idea was present to his mind, he could not help applying to you the Beautiful Epitaph, Mr. [Alexander] Pope wrote to the memory of his Friend Mr. Secretary [James] Cragg.

> Statesman yet Friend to truth, of Soul Sincere,
> In Action Faithful, and in Honor Clear!
> Who broke no Promise, Serv'd no Private end,
> Who gained no Title, and who lost no Friend,
> Ennobled by Himself, by all approved
> Praised, wept, and Honored, by the Muse he loved.

It was Unanimously, & Heartily agreed by this Respectable Company, that these Lines exhibited an Exact and perfect portrait of Coll. Hamilton's Character; The delight I felt at this Just and grateful Ulogium has prompted me to Communicate it to the only Gentleman, who will probably feel less Sensibility on the Occasion, than any of his Numerous Friends Though I presume, a Just Tribute of praise, which flows from a grateful sense of those great and essential Benefits, a man derives to this Country, by Superior abilities, and unremitting devotion to its real Interests, cannot be Ungrateful to the Genuine Donor himself.

ALEXANDER HAMILTON TO JEREMIAH OLNEY,
PHILADELPHIA, 2 APRIL 1793
[As secretary of the treasury Hamilton tells Providence, R.I., Customs Collector Olney not to be overly strict in collecting duties.] My own maxims of conduct are not favorable to much discretion, but cases do sometimes occur in which a little may be indispensable. The exercise of it must always be at the peril of the officer, and therefore ought to stand on manifest ground.

But wherever it should appear to have been discreetly and prudently exercised, upon an *urgent* occasion, due allowances would be made for it.

ALEXANDER HAMILTON TO ANDREW G. FRAUNCES,
PHILADELPHIA, 2 AUGUST 1793
Do you imagine that any menaces of appeal to the people can induce me to depart from what I conceive to be my public duty?

THOMAS JEFFERSON TO JAMES MADISON, PHILADELPHIA,
8 SEPTEMBER 1793
Hamilton is ill of the fever as is said. He had two physicians out at his house the night before last. His family think him in danger, & he puts himself so by his excessive alarm. He had been miserable several days before from a firm persuasion he should catch it [i.e., yellow fever]. A man as timid as he is on the water, as timid on horseback, as timid in sickness, would be a ph'nomenon if the courage of which he has the reputation in military occasions were genuine.

DEWITT CLINTON TO MISS CORNELIA CLINTON,
ALBANY, N.Y., 23 JANUARY 1794
... the two great financiers, i.e., the two great pests of the World—Hamilton and Pitt must now fall like Lucifer never to rise again.

JOHN NICHOLAS TO PRESIDENT GEORGE WASHINGTON,
6 APRIL 1794
It is rumoured in the city that you are about to send an Envoy to the court of Great Britain and that your choice will probably fall on the Secretary of the treasury—You will pardon me for saying that the measure in itself is improper because unnec-

essary and that when connected with the instrument it bodes infinite mischief to yourself and your country. . . .

I confess myself astonished to hear the nomination which is made for this office—at a time when perhaps more than half America have determined it to be unsafe to trust power in the hands of this person however remotely it is connected with many of the odious traits in his character—at a time when at least one half the legislature are afraid to exert themselves in the most trying situation of their country, lest his present powers should enable him to wrest them to purposes which he is supposed by them to entertain & which they dread more than the open attack of Great Britain—at a time when this person is the avowed friend of Great Britain in the most infamous contest, when all his measures have tended to throw this country into her arms & many entertain suspicion with some grounds that the present hostility of that country to this is partly intended to aid his well known attachment to it—to appoint him to an office in which he could immediately & successfully advance his purposes would be to stake the American happiness on the justice of one of two opinions where both are advocated by equal numbers—every man in a republic is a centinel on public safety and the warnings of danger should [be] listened to rather than the assurances of safety from the importance of the consequences which may follow—I confess my expectation was of a very different kind, that he who was elected to office by the love of the people would not exercise his power to the destruction of their happiness & is it less when he who is suffered to shares most of the authority of the government is suspected of undermining the public happiness—I may be told that these suspicions are groundless and that an equal number of men in America are strongly attached to him—both may be true & yet the injury remain unimpaired—if there are deep rooted prejudices which visibly gain strength is it not inhuman to continually resist them—if children are afraid of hobgoblins is it not unwise and cruel to cherish and alarm their fears—it is immaterial what is the truth unless it can be conveyed to our minds—let the rate of understanding be what it will men must be governed on an estimate of what it is & not what it might be—but he is supported by equal numbers—this if an argument at all will be found a strong one for his dismission—one side hopes an accession of good the other side the loss of all that is dear to them—is there an equality in these pretensions—there certainly would not be if the makers were unequal—the government no body will say depends on him—one half America determine that it will be ruined by him—In all governments it has been found necessary to consult the public opinion on the persons employed & it has ever been concluded that a continued favor to an unpopular servant ought to involve the master in the blame. In America this has not yet happened altho' I greatly fear it is rapidly in progress—the unexampled affection of the people to you requires more to shake their confidence than is usually necessary but natural causes must operate & it is a well known principle that small injuries obliterate important services—this is not contradicted by present experience, for there is rather a suspension of opinion than a disregard of wrong—the present moment may determine the mind & to be sure the love of our country will fully justify the decision—to put a drawn sword into the hands of a suspected madman is to expose every body in his way to ruin & when the mischief shall happen it will be a poor satisfaction to say you did not believe it—the affection of the people has hitherto prevented their blame of your measures from lessening their confidence in you, but it will be a poor return for what should excite your gratitude to persevere in what is disagreeable to them—the strongest affection cannot withstand injury whetted by insult—did it never occur to you that the divisions of America might be ended by the sacrafice of this one man—I do sincerely believe from my own knowledge of the causes of divisions & the obvious interest that his partizans have to unite in any mode of executing the government which will preserve its credit, that they would & to a heart solicitous for its country's happiness the event must be most desireable.

I have extended this subject to great length without saying half that occurs & indeed it was only my intention to have given a testimony to public opinion which you may perhaps not have heard—I aver it to be as I have stated it—the consequences must be obvious to you—if the mission should be unfortunate you will bear the undivided odium—if it should be successful it will do you no service, for the event will be too late to stop the opinion that you are determined to govern America according to your own inclination & that of one half its inhabitants and in contempt of the most rooted opinions of the other half—Among them at present you possess almost universal confidence & it should be rendered dear to you by the reflection that it has stood the conflict of opinions unaided by the smallest dependence on your influence—I myself am one of those who have hitherto shut my eyes on those events which could even shake my confidence in your discernment & I declare I shall meet the event with grief which will persuade me that you are no longer your country's bulwark.

Are you apprized of the clamour which is raised against the government by Mr. Morris being employed in a service for which his principles render him so unfit*—Mr. H. is understood to have the same wishes with respect to France & a position at London will be infinitely more favorable for their gratification than at Paris—faction has doubted whether you could be a friend to the revolutionary principle & throw such a stumbling block in its way—a second appointment of that sort will give distrust to every jealous defender of the right of self government.

Can you justify to America increasing the power of a man who is now under question for that which he already has? with so many objections to him will it not shew an excess of favoritism to appoint him to an office inconsistent with the duties of that which he already fills? May it not deserve consideration whether you can dispense with the exercise of official duty as you will do by sending the officer from America.

When the above was written it was my intention as you will perceive by the contents to have sent it without a signature & on one account I wished for concealment, but reflection tells me that I do justice neither to my principles nor present intentions in supposing that one or the other can be doubted— If the spirit in which it is written should be conveyed by it I shall have no reason to regret the want of those expressions of respect which I could honestly have mixed with my political opinions—If there is any information which I may be supposed to possess which is desireable to you I shall take pleasure in attending you

*A reference to Gouverneur Morris's appointment as U.S. minister to France.

ALEXANDER HAMILTON TO PRESIDENT GEORGE WASHINGTON, PHILADELPHIA, 8 APRIL 1794
Upon this as upon every other occasion my desire is to encounter directly and without detour whatever embarrassment may stand in my way.

JAMES MONROE TO PRESIDENT GEORGE WASHINGTON, PHILADELPHIA 11 APRIL 1794
My letter of the 8th, and to which I was on the succeeding day honored with a reply, was written in the belief that great

exertions were made to convince you that it was the general wish of the community Colo. Hamilton should be appointed Envoy extraordinary to G. Britain upon the present occasion. As I knew that this was not the case, but on the contrary was persuaded that a great majority of the people of America would not only disapprove the nomination, but deem it likely to produce much mischief, I thought it consistent with the duty I owed the publick, and that respect I have always personally entertained for you, to apprize you of it. A knowledge of truths and even of opinions upon this subject, might be serviceable & could not be injurious; and in point of propriety I could perceive no difference in communicating them, as well against, as for a nomination: otherwise indeed than as the latter is the more pleasant service to the person rendering it. I am therefore happy to find that the part I have taken in this respect, was received in that confidential & friendly manner it was intended, and shall accordingly proceed to state to you in writing the objections which have occurred against the nomination.

I am led to conclude from the liberal stile of your letter that you are willing I should state to you generally the objections which have been urged against it. Upon that principle this reply will be founded. In case however I have misapprehended your intention, I beg you to ascribe it to that consideration alone, and not to a desire to obtrude any opinions of mine upon you.

That there exists among us a party, not to be slighted for its talents or numbers strongly attached to the British monarchy & nation, is a fact which I presume no address has been able to hide from your view. The demonstration of such a party is to be trac'd from an early period of the government, and is to be found in its uniform partiality for both upon every occasion which occurred; in declarations innumerable both in publick & private; but above all in its constant & systematic enmity to the French nation & revolution, of which latter disposition, not to go further back, sufficient proof has been furnished during the present session alone.

This single consideration is sufficient to excite a suspicion of the views of this party. To patronize and support G. Britain when appearances would allow it, & when her dangerous projects are unmasked, & the publick mind wounded with accumulated injuries is inraged against her, and to discountenance France the friend and ally of America, in every instance, must have something in view unfriendly to the liberty & safety of these States.

That Colo. Hamilton is a member of this party, active in its councils and devoted to its interests is generally and well known. The particular proofs of it are numerous, positive, & satisfactory. The free disclosure of his sentiments upon these subjects, in conversations, anonymous publications (known however to be his) and in his intrigues, have pretty generally explained his true character to the publick. Tis manifest that at present his prospects are founded upon the British & monarchic interests here alone, and in proportion as the confidence of the country has been withdrawn from him, he has more entirely thrown himself upon the support of the former.

Should a person therefore of such character & principles be sent to England, and upon an occasion so attractive of the publick notice, it would not only furnish an opportunity for political intrigue against republicanism here, and against our connection with France, but as I have reason to believe, be regarded in America in a light, unfavorable to the authority appointing him. Nor could it fail to be viewed by France, in respect to the byas of our publick councils, otherwise than with the strongest jealousy and dissatisfaction. and if the mission should not succeed in its object, and a state of things ensue so as to require the friendship and co-operation of that country with this, our situation would be as mortifying as it would be alarming. nor could neither ask with propriety for aid, nor could she with pleasure grant it afterwards.

That an understanding subsists at the present time between this party and the British administration is not improbable and generally inferred, from the late communications of Mr. Pinckney. The footing of intimacy upon which it is known to stand with their minister here, is a circumstance which naturally cherishes the suspicion.*

That the views of this party have been latterly better understood by the community at large and its influence greatly diminished, is to be plainly seen, by the present state of the legislation. Indeed it is obvious that whenever any of those whose principles are best known, revolve back on their constituents, especially in the Senate, they are superseded. The publick mind is rapidly forcing its way in opposition to the views of this party and so far as a respect is due to that consideration a strong objection arises against the nomination.

*Thomas Pinckney was the U.S. minister plenipotentiary to Great Britain, and George Hammond was the British minister to the United States.

ALEXANDER HAMILTON TO PRESIDENT GEORGE
WASHINGTON, PHILADELPHIA, 14 APRIL 1794

Knowing as I do Sir that I am among the persons who have been in your contemplation to be employed in the capacity I have mentioned, I should not have taken the present step, had I not been resolved at the same time to advise you with decision to drop me from the consideration and to fix upon another character. I am not unapprised of what has been the byass of your opinion on the subject—I am well aware of all the collateral obstacles which exist—and I assure you in the utmost sincerity that I shall be completely and intirely satisfied with the election of another.

ABIGAIL ADAMS TO JOHN ADAMS, QUINCY, MASS.,
10 MAY 1794

I have ever thought with respect to that Man, "beware of that spair Cassius"—this might be done consistant with prudence, and without the illiberal abuse in many respects so plentifully cast upon him. The writers however discover too plainly that envy Pride and malice are the Sources from whence their opposition arrises, instead of the publick good.

ALEXANDER HAMILTON TO PRESIDENT GEORGE
WASHINGTON, ROSTRAVER TOWNSHIP, PA.,
11 NOVEMBER 1794

[Hamilton was suppressing the Whiskey Rebellion in western Pennsylvania.] It is long since I have learnt to hold popular opinion of no value. I hope to derive from the esteem of the discerning and in internal consciousnous of zealous endeavors for the public good the reward of those endeavors.

WILLIAM HETH TO ALEXANDER HAMILTON,
SHILLELAH, VA., 6 JULY 1794

[After Treasury Secretary Hamilton successfully withstood a hostile congressional investigation of his department.] Accept, I pray you, my dear friend, of my sincerest congratulations, on your second, and complete triumph, over the invidious persecutions of a base faction. The report of the Committee of Congress, has turned out precisely, as your friends here, had predicted—"The more you *probe*, examine, & investigate Hamilton's conduct; rely upon it, the *greater* he will appear." But it was a cruel thing in Congress, & some what unprecedented, I presume, to oblige your *persecutor, & prosecutors*, to sit as your *Judges*, and, what was more ill-natured, to compel them to make a *Report*: by which, they were obliged—d____d mortification, surely—to *convict* you, of purity of conduct, & unshaken integrity, and a constant watchfulness over the public interest. This was cursed hard upon them, to be sure. And how one of them [William Branch Giles] who had *pledged himself* to convict you of nothing less than *"high crimes & misdemeanors"* can get the better of his chagrin, or meet some of his credulous, & deluded constituents without shame & confusion, I am at a loss to account. Nothing surely, can carry him through, but that consummate vanity and ambition, which first tempted him to make so unprovoked, & so unwarrantable an Attack. He has been completely mortified, at a public-meeting, in his own District, since his return. Instead of entertaining all companies, as heretofore, with declamations on the abuses in The Treasury Department; not a single syllable was uttered about Hamilton, or his conduct. He was *"as mute as a fish."* No notice were taken of any of the toasts which *he* gave; while those given by [Edward] Carrington were *huzzad* and *applauded.*

JOHN ADAMS TO ABIGAIL ADAMS, PHILADELPHIA, 20 JANUARY 1795

Hamilton will do better [than Henry Knox in private life]. He is younger and has more Oeconomy. It is Said he refuses all public Employment and goes resolutely to the Bar at New York. He refuses to Stand Candidate for Governor.

PRESIDENT GEORGE WASHINGTON TO ALEXANDER HAMILTON, PHILADELPHIA, 2 FEBRUARY 1795

After so long an experience of your public services, I am naturally led, at this moment of your departure from office—which it has always been my wish to prevent—to review them.

In every relation, which you have borne to me, I have found that my confidence in your talents, exertions and integrity, has been well placed. I the more freely render this testimony of my approbation, because I speak from opportunities of information which cannot deceive me, and which furnish satisfactory proof of your title to public regard.

JAMES MCHENRY TO ALEXANDER HAMILTON,
NEAR BALTIMORE, MD., 17 FEBRUARY 1795

The tempest weathered and landed on the same shore I may now congratulate you upon have established a system of credit and having conducted the affairs of our country upon principles and reasoning which ought to insure its immortality as it undoubtedly will your fame. Few public men have been so eminently fortunate as voluntarily to leave so high a station with so unsullied a character and so well-assured a reputation, and still fewer have so well deserved the gratitude of their country and the elogiums of history. Let this console you for past toils and pains, and reconcile you to humble pleasures and a private life. What remains for you having ensured fame but to ensure felicity. Seek for it in the moderate pursuit of your profession, or if public life still flatters in that office most congenial to it, and which will not withdraw you from those literary objects that require no violent waste of spirits, and those little plans that involve gentle exercise and which you can drop or indulge in without injury to your family.

I have built houses, I have cultivated fields, I have planned gardens, I have planted trees, I have written little essays, I have made poetry once a year to please my wife, at times got children and at all times thought myself happy. Why cannot you do the same, for after all if a man is only to acquire fame or distinctions by continued privations and abuse I would incline to prefer a life of privacy and little pleasures.

ALEXANDER HAMILTON TO ROBERT TROUP, ALBANY, N.Y.,
13 APRIL 1795

If I cannot live *in splendor* in town with a moderate fortune acquired, I can at least live *in comfort* in the country, and I am content to do so.

WILLIAM BRADFORD TO ALEXANDER HAMILTON,
PHILADELPHIA, 2 JULY 1795

It will always give me pleasure to hear from you: & I will endeavor to repay you with what you may consider "as a smack of the Whip." Yet I hear that you have renounced every thing but your profession—that you will not even pick up money when it lies at your feet, unless it comes in the form of a fee! But it is in vain to kick against the pricks. You were made for a Statesman, & politics will never be out of your head.

THOMAS JEFFERSON TO JAMES MADISON, MONTICELLO,
21 SEPTEMBER 1795

Hamilton is really a colossus to the antirepublican party. Without numbers, he is an host within himself. They have got themselves into a defile, where they might be finished; but too much security on the Republican part, will give time to his talents & indefatigableness to extricate them. We have had only middling performances to oppose him. In truth, when he comes forward, there is nobody but yourself who can meet him. His adversaries having begun the attack, he has the advantage of answering them, & remains unanswered himself. . . . For god's sake take up your pen, and give a fundamental reply to Curtius & Camillus.

WILLIAM HETH TO ALEXANDER HAMILTON, VIRGINIA,
11 JANUARY 1796

[Writing in the third person, Heth says] he does not blush to say, that he loves you as a private friend, admires you as an able & most faithful public servant; and venerates you as a Man of most superior talents.

JOHN ADAMS TO ABIGAIL ADAMS, PHILADELPHIA,
27 FEBRUARY 1796

Two great Political Questions have been agitated in the supream Court. One about Virginia Debts paid into the Treasury—the other the Constitutionality of the Carriage Tax. Hamilton argued this last for three hours with his usual Splendor of Talents & Eloquence as they say. In the Course of his argument he said no Man was obliged to pay the Tax. This he knew by Experiment: for after having enjoyed the Pleasure of riding in his Carriage for six years he had been obliged to lay it down and was happy.

ALEXANDER HAMILTON TO PRESIDENT GEORGE
WASHINGTON, NEW YORK, 5 SEPTEMBER 1796

Had I had *health* enough, it was my intention to have written it [i.e., Washington's farewell Address] over, in which case I could both have improved & abridged. But this is not the case. I seem now to have regularly a period of ill health every summer.

JOHN ADAMS TO ABIGAIL ADAMS, PHILADELPHIA,
9 JANUARY 1797

Hamilton I know to be a proud Spirited, conceited, aspiring Mortal always pretending to Morality, with as debauched Morals as old Franklin who is more his Model than any one I know. As great an Hypocrite as any in the U.S. His Intrigues in the Election I despise. That he has Talents I admit. But I dread none of them. I shall take no notice of his Puppyhood but retain the same Opinion of him I always had and maintain the Same Conduct towards him I always did, that is keep him at a distance.

ABIGAIL ADAMS TO JOHN ADAMS, QUINCY, MASS.,
28 JANUARY 1797

Mr. [Moses] Black told me the other Day on his return from Boston, that Col. H_____ was loosing ground with his Friends in Boston. On what account I inquired. Why for the part he is Said to have acted in the late Election. Aya what was that? Why they say that he tried to keep out both Mr. A[dam]s and J[efferso]n, and that he behaved with great Duplicity. He wanted to bring in Pinckney that he himself might be the Dictator—So you See according to the old adage, Murder will out. I despise a Janus tho I do not feel a disposition to rail at or condemn the conduct of those who did not vote for you, because it is my firm belief that if the people had not been imposed upon by false reports and misrepresentations, the vote would have been nearly unanimous—H__n dared not risk his popularity to come out openly in opposition, but he went Secretly cunningly as he thought to work, and as his influence is very great in the N England States, he imposed upon them. [Fisher] Ames you know has been his firm Friend. I do not believe he suspected him, nor [George] Cabot neither whom I believe he play'd upon—[William] Smith of S.C. was Duped by him I suspect.

Beware of that Spair Cassius, has always occured to me when I have seen that cock Sparrow. O I have read his Heart in his Wicked Eyes many a time the very Devil is in them. They are laciviousness itself, or I have no Skill in Phisiognomy.

ABIGAIL ADAMS TO CHARLES ADAMS, QUINCY, MASS.,
5 FEBRUARY 1797

There is a Character in your state who with all his pretensions to Friendship, took a very ungenerous part in the late Elections.

Tho he thought to conceal himself under that Mask, the covering has been Seen through, and his real views and Motives discovered. He may have superiour talents to Jefferson, but he has not half his disinterested Friendship—the Gentleman I mean was not a Candidate for either office. He is one however upon whom I placed my Eye very early, nor do I mean to withdraw it whilst I am an observer. "Beware of that Spair Cassius" this is between ourselves.—

ABIGAIL ADAMS TO THOMAS BOYLSTON ADAMS,
PHILADELPHIA, 3 JANUARY 1798

There has been *one other* Book written by a Gentleman formerly in publick office,* but as I do not wish to circulate scandle, I shall not send it you. I dare Vouch for it, your Brother has had it, or accounts of it.

Some persons have given it the title of "whose's the Dupe." Others of a more proflicate turn have quoted the old saw, of the greatest sin this side [of] Hell, is first to kiss and then to tell; but confessions have not washd the Ethiope white, nor at all cleard up the publick transactions, which stood fair and unshaken, by the disclosure of a private Amour, alass—alass—how weak is Humane Nature.

*Alexander Hamilton's *Observations* . . . (1797) in which he responded to charges of "improper pecuniary speculation" claiming that he was blackmailed by the husband of his mistress.

THOMAS BOYLSTON ADAMS TO ABIGAIL ADAMS,
BERLIN, GERMANY, 12 FEBRUARY 1798

The *one other* book to which you allude, has, as you conjectured, already reached us. I hardly know what to say of it, though by the rules of gallantry I should pronounce the hero guilty of a notorious breach therein; for his awkward management and want of address. The *benefit* of telling one's own story in these cases, is not much to be courted. The *ladies* never forgive *that* crime. It admits of no apology, and whoever is reduced to the extremity of confession must suffer all the consequences of such an offence.—But there are different grades in vice, and in the opinion of *every man*, the outrage of the ex-Secretary upon public decorum, bears no comparison with the behaviour of those who extorted it from him. Has not the man, who has published a book of 406 pages, betrayed confidence also, divulged secrets of State, infinitely momentous in comparison of a paltry amour? Has he not discovered upon every occasion since his return a malign spirit, a base temper, fit only for a Devil or one of the *Illuminati*? What sentiment of honor or morality can possess that man's mind, that has not pride or generosity enough to sacrifice a resentment to a sense of public good but will rather expose to the enemies of his Country those sacred secrets deposited with him, while he was employed in its service? God be praised there are no more such Ministers from the United States in Europe, nor is there more than *one man* in our Government at home, liable to be seized with the distemper, so common among his neighbors & intimates, that of betraying their Country's trust.

TIMOTHY PICKERING TO GEORGE WASHINGTON,
PHILADELPHIA, 6 JULY 1798
[Considering the appointment of officers to lead the U.S. provisional army.] There is one man who will gladly be *Your Second*; but who will not, I presume, because I think he ought not to be, the Second to any other military commander in the U. States. You too well know Colo. Hamilton's distinguished ability, energy and fidelity, to apply my remark to any other man. But to ensure his appointment, I apprehend the weight of your opinion may be necessary. From the conversation that I and others have had with the President [i.e., John Adams],

there appears to us to be a disinclination to place Colo. Hamilton in what we think is his proper station, and that alone in which we suppose he will serve—the *Second* to You—and the *Chief in your absence*. In any war, and especially in such a war as now impends, a Commander in Chief ought to know and have a confidence in the officers most essential to ensure success to his measures. In a late conversation with the president, I took the liberty to observe that the army in question not being yet raised, the only material object to be contemplated in the early appointment of the Commander in Chief, would be, that he might be consulted, because he ought to be satisfied, in the choice of the principal officers who serve under him.

If any considerations should prevent your taking the command of the army, I deceive myself extremely, if you will not think it should be conferred on Colo. Hamilton, and in this case, it might be equally important as in the former that you should intimate your opinion to the President. Even Colo. Hamilton's political enemies, I believe, would repose more confidence in him than in any military character that can be placed in competition with him.

GEORGE WASHINGTON TO PRESIDENT JOHN ADAMS,
MOUNT VERNON, VA., 25 SEPTEMBER 1798
It is an invidious task, at all times, to draw comparisons, and I shall avoid it as much as possible; but I have no hesitation in declaring, that if the Public is to be deprived of the Services of Colonel Hamilton in the Military line, that the Post he was destined to fill will not be easily supplied; and that this is the sentiment of the Public, I think I can venture to pronounce. Although Colonel Hamilton has never acted in the character of a General Officer, yet his opportunities, as the principal & most confidential aid of the Commander in chief, afforded him

the means of viewing every thing on a larger scale than those whose attentions were confined to Divisions or Brigades; who knew nothing of the correspondences of the Commander in Chief, or of the various orders to, or transactions with, the General Staff of the Army. These advantages, and his having served with usefulness in the Old Congress; in the General Convention; and having filled one of the most important departments of Government with acknowledged abilities and integrity, has placed him on high ground; and made him a conspicuous character in the United States, and even in Europe. To these, as a matter of no small consideration may be added, that as a lucrative practice in the line of his Profession is his most certain dependence, the inducement to relinquish it, must, in some degree, be commensurate. By some he is considered as an ambitious man, and therefore a dangerous one. That he is ambitious I shall readily grant, but it is of that laudable kind which prompts a man to excel in whatever he takes in hand. He is enterprising, quick in his perceptions, and his judgment intuitively great; qualities essential to a great military character, and therefore I repeat, that his loss will be irreparable.

GEORGE CABOT TO TIMOTHY PICKERING,
BROOKLINE, MASS., 17 NOVEMBER 1798
I lament with you the misfortune of Knox on his own account, and, I am sorry to add, on that of the public; for already he begins to intimate, though obscurely, that Hamilton is a man of insatiable ambition and not to be trusted.

ALEXANDER HAMILTON TO ELIZABETH HAMILTON,
PHILADELPHIA, 10 DECEMBER 1798
I cannot make everybody else as rapid as myself.

ABIGAIL ADAMS TO JOHN ADAMS, QUINCY, MASS.,
21 DECEMBER 1798

I enclose you my paper of yesterday. There is a foolish Eulogium upon H———n. I wish people would understand Characters more thoroughly before they worship them.

ABIGAIL ADAMS TO JOHN ADAMS, QUINCY, MASS.,
12 JANUARY 1799

The Idea which prevails here, is that Hamilton will be first in command, as there is very little Idea that Washington will be any thing more than, Name as to actual Service, and I am told that it ill suits the N. England Stomach. They say He is not a Native, and besides He has so damned himself to everlasting Infamy, that He ought not to be Head of any thing. The Jacobins Hate him and the Federalists do not Love him. Serious people are mortified, and every Uriah must tremble for his Bathsheba.

ABIGAIL ADAMS TO JOHN ADAMS, QUINCY, MASS.,
13 JANUARY 1799

I would however as soon trust Col. S^{he} [William Stephens Smith] as Genl. Hamilton. I have not any Confidence in the honor, integrity or patriotism of any Man, who does not believe that Thus shalt not commit Adultery is a positive prohibition of God. Thou shalt not covet thy Neighbor's wife, is an other, and yet I have been credibly informed that the Audacious publication of that Man has only rendered him more bold, and hardened in iniquity. It only requires a temptation sufficiently powerful to Ambition to lead from the path of political Rectitude; it is a strange way of Reasoning. I would not upon any consideration do a publick wrong or injury, but I can be guilty of breaking the most solemn private engagement and that to one whom I am bound by affection, and by Honor to protect, to Love and Respect. I can disgrace and stigmatize my Lawful offspring, and feel neither Shame or compunction, but I would not betray a public trust. I cannot see that I commit any breach of Charity in this comment.

ALEXANDER HAMILTON TO HENRY KNOX, NEW YORK, 14 MARCH 1799
... my heart advises otherwise and my heart has always been the Master of my Judgment.

JAMES WILKINSON TO ALEXANDER HAMILTON, NEW YORK, 16 AUGUST 1799
[Quoting a letter he wrote to James McHenry] "In the mean time permit me to refer you to Col. Hamilton, for his Opinion on the subject, as I consider Him the ablest military Judge of our Country; this opinion is not founded on any personal Intimacy with Col. H. but is the result of information on which I can rely."

ALEXANDER HAMILTON TO JOSIAH OGDEN HOFFMAN, NEW YORK, 6 NOVEMBER 1799
It is well known that I have long been the object of the most malignant calumnies of the faction opposed to our government through the medium of the papers devoted to their views.

Hitherto I have foreborne to resort to the laws for the punishment of the authors or abettors; and were I to consult personal considerations alone I should continue in this course, repaying hatred with contempt. But public motives now compel me to a different conduct. The design of that faction to overturn our government, and with it the great pillars of social security and happiness, in this country, become every day more manifest, and have of late acquired a degree of system, which renders them formidable. One principal Engine for effecting the scheme is by audacious falsehoods to destroy the confidence of the people in all those who are in any degree conspicuous among the supporters of the Government: an Engine which has been employed in time past with too much success, and which unless counteracted in future is likely to be attended with very fatal consequences. To counter act it is therefore a duty to the community.

ALEXANDER HAMILTON TO ELIZABETH HAMILTON,
ALBANY, N.Y., 16 JANUARY 1800
It is absolutely necessary to me when absent to hear frequently of you and my dear Children. While all other passions decline in me, those of love and friendship gain new strength. It will be more and more my endeavor to abstract myself from all pursuits which interfere with those of Affection. Tis here only I can find true pleasure. In this I know your good and kind heart responses to mine.

PHILADELPHIA *AURORA*, 1 MARCH 1800
... after he became governor Mr. [Henry] Lee in his free suavid mode soon forgot his political enmity—Hamilton *never* forgets.

ALEXANDER HAMILTON TO ELIZABETH HAMILTON,
SCOTCH PLAINS, NEW JERSEY, 24 MAY 1800
I am under a necessity of playing the game of good spirits, but separated from those I love, it is a most artificial game, and at the bottom of my soul there is a more than usual gloom.

JAMES MCHENRY TO ALEXANDER HAMILTON, WAR DEPT.,
WASHINGTON, D.C., 31 MAY 1800
[Recollections of a conversation between Secretary of War McHenry and President John Adams on May 5, 1800] President Adams: Hamilton is an intriguant—the greatest intriguant in the World—a man devoid of every moral principle—

a Bastard, and as much a foreigner as Gallatin. Mr. Jefferson is an infinitely better man, a wiser one, I am sure, and, if President, will act wisely. I know it, and would rather be Vice President under him, or even Minister Resident at the Hague, than indebted to such a being as Hamilton for the Presidency.

WILLIAM NORTH TO ALEXANDER HAMILTON, NEW YORK, 15 JUNE 1800
To you, my dear General, all eyes, look, & on you, everything will depend in a great measure, & as you are amongst the saints, it will not be improper to cite a text of scripture, "Be wise as serpents harmless as doves."* Your head is always right, I would, your heart was a little less susceptible. I pray you, when it is about to carry you out of the direct path, you will, like the deacons & Select men, throw a cloak over your shoulders.

You will consider this as a letter, not from an adjutant General to his Commander in chief, but from a citizen, a plain, private Citizen, who is anxious for the welfare of his country, & for the personal happiness of the man who under heaven, he hopes will one day, save that country from ruin.
*Matthew 10:16.

JOHN RUTLEDGE, JR., TO ALEXANDER HAMILTON, NEWPORT, R.I., 17 JULY 1800
I find the people in general very much devoted to Mr. Adams, from the mere circumstance I believe of his being an eastern man, & at the same time jealous & suspicious of you in the extreme.

ALEXANDER HAMILTON TO WILLIAM JACKSON. NEW YORK, 26 AUGUST 1800
The truth is that on the question of who my parents were, I have better pretensions than most of those who in this country plume themselves on ancestry.

JAMES MCHENRY TO ALEXANDER HAMILTON,
BALTIMORE, MD., 4 SEPTEMBER 1800

I sincerely believe that there is not one of your friends who have paid the least attention to the insinuations attempted to be cast on the legitimacy of your birth, or who would care or respect you less were all that your enemies say or impune on this head true. I think it will be most prudent and magnanimous to leave any explanation on the subject to your biographer, and the discretion of those friends to whom you have communicated the facts.

JOHN BECKLEY TO EPHRAIM KIRBY, 25 OCTOBER 1800

The turbulent and intriguing spirit of Alexander Hamilton, has again manifested itself, in an insidious publication* to defeat Mr. Adams's election, and in a labored effort to belittle the character of the president, he has in no small degree belittled his own. Vainly does he essay to seize the mantle of Washington, and cloak the moral atrocities of a life spent in wickedness and which must terminate in shame and dishonor. His career of ambition is passed, and neither honor or empire will ever be his. As a political nullity, he has inflicted upon himself the sentence of *"Aut Caesar, aut Nullus."***

*Letter Concerning the Public Conduct and Character of John Adams (October 1800).
**Either Caesar or nothing; either first or nothing.

JEDIDIAH MORSE TO OLIVER WOLCOTT, JR.,
27 OCTOBER 1800

The division among the Federalists, occasioned by the unfortunate Mission to France, & greatly increased by subsequent & corresponding measures, is a most serious calamity; & what will be the issue cannot be foreseen. Gen. Hamilton's Letter on the conduct & character of the President, which is circulating (rather privately however) among us, I fear will not mitigate, but increase the evil. It will administer *oil* rather than *water* to the fire. I can only lament (as I do most sincerely) the conduct that provoked the publication, & the too great warmth that dictated some parts of it. Of the patriotism & integrity of Genl. H. I have never entertained a doubt. He has talents of which any country might well be proud—but of his *prudence* in a former publication,* & in the present, many good men will have their doubts.... But in such cases, & concerning such a man, it will be a long time before the body of the people will form a correct judgment.

*A 1797 pamphlet in which Hamilton defended his actions as secretary of the treasury but admitted to an extra-marital affair.

ABIGAIL ADAMS TO MARY CRANCH, PHILADELPHIA,
10 NOVEMBER 1800

I shall not say any thing to you upon political subjects, no not upon the little Gen'l's Letter but reserve it for a future Letter when I arrive at Washington and you have more health to laugh at the folly, and pity the weakness, vanity and ambitious views of, as very a sparrow as Sterne commented upon, in his Sentimental Journey, or More describes in his fables.

GEORGE CABOT TO ALEXANDER HAMILTON,
BROOKLINE, MASS., 29 NOVEMBER 1800

I am *bound* to tell you that you are accused by respectable men of Egotism, & some very worthy & sensible men say you have exhibited the same *vanity* in your book which you charge as a dangerous quality & great weakness in Mr. Adams.

JOHN ADAMS TO DR. OGDEN, WASHINGTON, D.C.,
3 DECEMBER 1800

This last pamphlet [Hamilton's attack on Adams] I regret more on account of its author than on my own, because I am confident it will do him more harm than me. I am not his enemy, and never was. I have not adored him, like his idolaters, and have had great cause to disapprove of some of his politics. He has talents, if he would correct himself, which might be useful. There is more burnish, however, on the outside, than sterling silver in the substance.

ROBERT TROUP TO RUFUS KING, NEW YORK,
31 DECEMBER 1800

The current of public opinion still sets strongly against the discretion of Hamilton's late letter respecting the character and conduct of Mr. Adams. I do not believe it has altered a single vote in the late election. . . . The influence however of this letter upon Hamilton's character is extremely unfortunate. An opinion has grown out of it, which at present obtains almost universally, that his character *is radically deficient in discretion*, and therefore the Federalists ask, what avail the most preeminent talents—the most distinguished patriotism—without the all important quality of discretion? Hence he is considered as an unfit head of the party—and we are in fact without a rallying point.

GOUVERNEUR MORRIS TO ALEXANDER HAMILTON,
WASHINGTON, D.C., 5 JANUARY 1801

You who are temperate in drinking have never perhaps noticed the awkward Situation of a Man who continues to be sober after the Company are drunk.

JOHN ADAMS TO THOMAS BOYLSTON ADAMS,
WASHINGTON, JANUARY 24, 1801

The Adherents of Mr. Hamilton, excepting a part of the Officers of the Cincinnati, are chiefly the Old Tories and their Connections. These have trumpeted and puffed his Talents, his Integrity and his disinterestedness these twenty years. They all ever hated Hancock and Samuel Adams, and although they have affected an Appearance of Some complaisance to me, in Consequence of my known principles and projects of Government, they have never loved me in their hearts. Their extravagant Praises of Washington have been merely to divert praises from Hancock's and Adams's and McKean's &c on one hand and to boost the heavy Christian Hamilton up upon Washington's fame, on the other.

JOHN QUINCY ADAMS TO WILLIAM VANS MURRAY,
BERLIN, GERMANY, 27 JANUARY 1801
As for the man, I too have always had a very high opinion of his talents and of his services. His system of finance I did consider as more complicated than was necessary, and the purity of his principles from frailties of *ambition* as not absolutely unquestionable. The rancor and the baseness of the means exerted against him by his enemies and rivals gave his merit an additional value and a stronger claim to support. Perhaps these rivals hurt in a way even unexpected to themselves. Perhaps by using infamous weapons against him they habituated his mind to consider the employment of them as warrantable. This degradation of soul, which you so justly describe in one of your late letters as the too natural result of our newspaper electioneering altercations, is to such a character as Hamilton's a greater injury, than all the charges that envy or malice under the mask of public spirit were ever able to conjure against him.

ALEXANDER HAMILTON TO GOUVERNEUR MORRIS,
NEW YORK, 29 FEBRUARY 1802
Mine is an odd destiny. Perhaps no man in the U States has sacrificed or done more for the present Constitution than myself, and contrary to all my anticipations of its fate, as you

know from the very beginning, I am still laboring to prop the frail and worthless fabric. Yet I have the murmurs of its friends no less than the curses of its foes for my rewards. What can I do better than withdraw from the scene? Every day proves to me more and more that the American world was not made for me.

ROBERT TROUP TO RUFUS KING, NEW YORK, 9 APRIL 1802
Hamilton is closely pursuing the law, and I have at length succeeded in making him somewhat mercenary. I have known him latterly to dun his clients for money, and in settling an account with me the other day, he reminded me that I had received a fee for him in settling a question referred to him and me jointly. These indications of regard to property give me hopes that we shall not be obliged to raise a subscription to pay for his funeral expenses.

ROBERT TROUP TO RUFUS KING, NEW YORK, 6 JUNE 1802
The fatigue occasioned by the constant sitting of our courts exhausted us all very much. I find that Hamilton's health, notwithstanding the quickness and enormous strength of his mind, is impairing, as well as mine. This man's mind, by the by, seems to be progressing to greater and greater maturity; such is the common opinion of our bar; and I may say with truth that his powers are now enormous! and the only chance we have of success is now and then when he happens to be on the weaker side: and yet he is always complaining that he does not get his share of judgments and decrees!

ROBERT TROUP TO RUFUS KING, NEW YORK,
24 AUGUST 1802
No mortal can yet calculate the present state of public opinion. Federalism is looking up. At the last 4th of July the toasts

everywhere given prove that Hamilton is regaining that general esteem and confidence, which he seems to have lost, and his standing is very much our political thermometer.

ALEXANDER HAMILTON TO RICHARD PETERS, NEW YORK,
29 DECEMBER 1802
A disappointed politician you know is very apt to take refuge in a garden.

RUFUS KING TO CHRISTOPHER GORE, NEW YORK,
20 NOVEMBER 1803
Hamilton is at the head of his profession, and in the annual receipt of a handsome income. He lives wholly at his house 9 miles from town so that on an average he must spend three hours a day on the road going and returning between his house and town, which he performs four or five days each week. I don't perceive that he meddles or feels much concerning Politics. He has formed very decided opinions of our System as well as of our administration, and as the one and the other has the voice of the country, he has nothing to do but to prophecy!

ALEXANDER HAMILTON: STATEMENT ON THE
IMPENDING DUEL WITH AARON BURR, NEW YORK,
28 JUNE–10 JULY 1804
My religious and moral principles are strongly opposed to the practice of dueling, and it would even give me pain to be obliged to shed the blood of a fellow creature in a private combat forbidden by the laws.

ALEXANDER HAMILTON: EXPLANATION OF FINANCIAL
SITUATION, NEW YORK, 1 JULY 1804
My public labors have amounted to an absolute sacrifice of the interests of my family.

ALEXANDER HAMILTON TO ELIZABETH HAMILTON,
NEW YORK, 4 JULY 1804

This letter, my very dear Eliza, will not be delivered to you, unless I shall first have terminated my earthly career, to begin, as I humbly hope, from redeeming grace and divine mercy, a happy immortality.

GOUVERNEUR MORRIS: EULOGY, NEW YORK, JULY 1804

Students of Columbia—he was in the ardent pursuit of knowledge in your academic shades, when the first sound of the American war called him to the field. A young and unprotected volunteer, such was his zeal and so brilliant his service that we heard his name before we knew his person—It seemed as if God had called him suddenly into existence, that he might assist to save a world! ...

He disdained concealment. Knowing the purity of his heart, he bore it as it were in his hand, exposing to every passenger its inmost recesses....

His unsuspecting confidence in professions which he believed to be sincere, led him to trust too much to the undeserving. This exposed him to misrepresentation....

Oh! my fellow citizens, remember this solemn testimonial, that he was not ambitious. Yet, he was charged with ambition; and wounded by the Imputation, when he laid down his command, he declared, in the proud independence of his soul that he never would accept of any office, unless in a foreign war he should be called on to expose his life in defence of his country. This determination was immovable. It was his fault that his resolutions could not be changed. Knowing his own firm purpose, he was indignant at the charge that he sought for place or power. He was ambitious only of glory, but he was deeply solicitous for you. For himself he feared nothing, but he feared that bad men might, by false professions, acquire your confidence and abuse it to your ruin.

BENJAMIN RUSH: COMMONPLACE BOOK, 12 JULY 1804
Died of a wound received in a duel the day before from Col. Burr, Alexander Hamilton, Esq., the Aid of Washington in the field and his principal councillor in the Cabinet while President of the United States. He was learned, ingenious, and eloquent, and the object of universal admiration and attachment of one party, and of hatred of the other party which then constituted the American people. He was greatly and universally lamented. Funeral orations were delivered in honor of him in New York and Boston, and funeral sermons were preached upon his death in many churches. Mourning was worn for him by many of the citizens of the principal cities and towns in the United States.

GEORGE CABOT TO JOHN LOWELL, BOSTON, 18 JULY 1804
Newspapers of the day . . . will announce and explain to you the public misfortune experienced here by the untimely death of Hamilton. You know how well his friends loved him, and all esteemed him. You can therefore judge of the general sensibility at his death. I have always thought his virtues surpassed those of other men almost as his talents. His errors, unfortunately for the country, were conspicuous, and diminished his influence, which otherwise would have been irresistible, and was always directed to the noblest purposes. All reflecting men seem now to be sensible that he was our *hope* in the crisis to which our affairs necessarily drive us.

JOHN ADAMS: AUTOBIOGRAPHY
Of Hamilton, when he came into the General's Family I need say nothing. For my Part I never heard of him till after the Peace, and the Evacuation of the City of New York. The World has heard enough of him since. His Petulance, Impertinence and Impudence, will make too great a figure in these memories hereafter.

JOHN ADAMS: AUTOBIOGRAPHY

Here again the Honesty of Hamilton appears. The Articles of War and the Institution of the Army during the War, were all my Work, and yet he represents me as an Enemy to a regular Army. Although I have long since forgiven this Arch Enemy, yet Vice, Folly and Villainy are not to be forgotten, because the guilty Wretch repented, in his dying Moments. Although David repented, We are no where commanded to forget the Affair of Uriah: though the Magdalene reformed, We are not obliged to forget her former *Vocation*: though the Thief on the cross was converted, his Felony is still upon Record. The Prodigal Son repented and was forgiven, yet his Harlots and riotous living, and even the Swine and the husks that brought him to consideration, cannot be forgotten. Nor am I obliged by any Principles of Morality or Religion to suffer my Character to lie under infamous Calumnies, because the Author of them, with a Pistol Bullet through his Spinal Marrow, died a Penitent. Charity requires that We should hope and believe that his humiliation was sincere, and I hope he was forgiven: but I will not conceal his former Character at the Expense of so much Injustice to my own, as this Scottish Creolian Bolingbroke in the days of his disappointed Ambition and unbridled Malice and revenge, was pleased falsely to attempt against it. Born on a Speck more obscure than Corsica, from an Original not only contemptible but infamous, with infinitely less courage and Capacity than Bonaparte, he would in my Opinion, if I had not controlled the fury of his Vanity, instead of relieving this Country from Confusion as Bonaparte did France, he would have involved it in all the Bloodshed and distractions of foreign and civil War at once.

JOHN ADAMS TO BENJAMIN RUSH, QUINCY, MASS., 7 JULY 1805

Every state in the union has a party... who are still Englishmen in their hearts and will afford a mere American no support.

These factions . . . have made it a fixed principle all along to hunt down every true American and every revolutionary character as soon as they possibly could and get them out of their way. They were all, in one of these parties, taught to turn their eyes for this purpose upon that Scottish Creole, Alexander Hamilton, as their head, and what he was to do with them or what they were to do with him I will not at present conjecture; but I have an opinion which may one day be developed. Probably it went no further than an alliance with England and an alienation from France, without well considering what must have been the necessary effect of such a plan.

JOHN ADAMS TO BENJAMIN RUSH, QUINCY, MASS., 23 AUGUST 1805

You rank Colonel Hamilton among the Revolutionary characters. But why? The Revolution had its beginning, its middle, and its end before he had anything to do in public affairs. Col. Reed, Col. Harrison, and Mr. Edmund Randolph were secretaries to general Washington before Hamilton was in his family. . . . I never knew that such a man or boy was in his suite, nor did I ever hear the name of Hamilton till after the evacuation of New York [November 1783]; this boy came forward a bawling advocate for the Tories. . . .

You say that Washington and Hamilton are idolized by the tories. Hamilton is; Washington is not. To speak the truth, they puffed Washington like an air balloon to raise Hamilton into the air. Their preachers, their orators, their pamphlets and newspapers have spoken out and avowed publicly since Hamilton's death what I very well knew to be in their hearts for many years before, viz: that Hamilton was everything and Washington but a name. . . .

Hamilton's talents have been greatly exaggerated. His knowledge of the great subjects of coin and commerce and their intimate connections with all departments of every government, especially such as are so elective as ours, was very superficial and imperfect. He had derived most of his information from [William] Duer, who was a brother-in-law of Mr. Rose, the deputy secretary of the treasury under Mr. Pitt. Duer had long been secretary to the board of treasury. [Arthur] Lee, [Samuel] Osgood, and [Walter] Livingston were all men of abilities and kept the books of the treasury in good order.... [Oliver] Wolcott's indefatigable industry with a seven year's experience at the Connecticut pay table came in aid of Hamilton and Duer, so that I see no extraordinary reason for so much exclusive glory to Hamilton.

GOUVERNEUR MORRIS TO AARON OGDEN,
28 DECEMBER 1805
Our poor friend Hamilton bestrode his hobby [i.e., a monarchical government], to the great annoyance of his friends and not without injury to himself. More a theoretic than a practical man, he was not sufficiently convinced that a system may be good in itself and bad in relation to particular circumstances. He well knew that his favorite form was inadmissible, unless as the result of civil war, and I suspect that his belief in that which he called an approaching crisis arose from a conviction that the kind of government most suitable, in his opinion, to this extensive country, could be established in no other way.

JOHN ADAMS TO BENJAMIN RUSH, QUINCY, MASS.,
25 JANUARY 1806
Although I read with tranquility and suffered to pass without animadversion in silent contempt the base insinuations of vanity and a hundred lies besides published in a pamphlet against me by an insolent coxcomb who rarely dined in good company, where there was good wine, without getting silly

and vaporing about his administration like a young girl about her brilliants and trinkets, yet I lose all patience when I think of a bastard brat of a Scottish pedlar daring to threaten to undeceive the world in their judgment of Washington by writing an history of his battles and campaigns. This creature was in a delirium of ambition; he had been blown up with vanity by the tories, had fixed his eyes on the highest station in America, and he hated every man, young or old, who stood in his way or could in any manner eclipse his laurels or rival his pretensions.

WILLIAM PLUMER MEMORANDUM, 15 MARCH 1806
That Hamilton was a great man—a great lawyer—a man of integrity—very ambitious—& was very anxious to effect, that ruinous measure, a *consolidation of the States*.

JOHN ADAMS TO BENJAMIN RUSH, QUINCY, MASS., 11 NOVEMBER 1806
The very same principle that influences a bully, to break the Windows of a whore that has jilted him, naturally stirrs up a great Prince to raise mighty Armies, and dream of nothing but seiges, battles and Victories. In this plan I cannot avoid introducing a reflection by Way of digression. What a pity it is that our Congress had not known this discovery, and that Alexander Hamilton's project of raising an Army of fifty thousand Men, ten thousand of them to be Cavalry and his projects of Sedition Laws and Alien Laws and of new Taxes to support his army, all arose from a superabundance of secretions which he could not find Whores enough to draw off? and that the same Vapours produced his Lyes and Slanders by which he totally destroyed his party forever and finally lost his Life in the field of honor.

Descriptions of Alexander Hamilton

JOHN ADAMS TO BENJAMIN RUSH, QUINCY, MASS.,
SEPTEMBER 1807

Hamilton had great disadvantages. His origin was infamous; his place of birth and education were foreign countries; his fortune was poverty itself; the profligacy of his life—his fornications, adulteries, and his incests—were propagated far and wide. Nevertheless, he "affich'd"* disinterestedness as boldly as Washington. His myrmidons asserted it with as little shame, though not a man of them believed it. All the rest of the world ridiculed and despised the pretext. He had not, therefore, the same success. Yet he found means to fascinate some and intimidate others. You and I know him also to have been an intriguer.

*advertised.

JOHN ADAMS TO BENJAMIN RUSH, QUINCY, MASS.,
25 FEBRUARY 1808

At the time of Hamilton's death, the Federal papers avowed that Hamilton was the soul and Washington the body, or in other words that Washington was the painted wooden head of the ship and Hamilton the pilot and steersman.

BENJAMIN RUSH TO JOHN ADAMS, PHILADELPHIA,
13 JULY 1808

I have lately heard that a life of General Hamilton is preparing for the press. It will consist of many documents which will throw light upon the councils of the army and government of the United States during the time Mr. Hamilton acted as aide-de-camp and secretary of the treasury under General Washington. One of Hamilton's friends said in my presence a few days ago, "the intended publication would show General W.

to be a *good* man but General Hamilton to be a *great* man." Let this work end as it will, I shall continue to believe that "great men are a lie, and mean men vanity,"* and that there is very little difference in that superstition which leads us to believe in what the world call "great men" and in that which leads us to believe in witches and conjurors.

*Psalms 62:9.

JOHN ADAMS TO THE *BOSTON PATRIOT*, 12 MAY 1809
Thus it is when Self Sufficient Ignorance, impertinently obtrudes itself into offices and Departments in which it has no Right nor colour nor pretense to interfere. Thus it is when ambition undertakes to Sacrifice all Characters and the Peace of Nations to its private Interest.

JOHN ADAMS TO JOSEPH WARD, QUINCY, MASS.,
SEPTEMBER 27, 1809
Hamilton was indeed a most fortunate and a most unfortunate Man. He had Talents and insinuating qualities; but he was a crafty designing Man with more Ambition than Principle, more Enterprize than Judgment.

I am very glad they have republished his Pamphlet. I intended to have proposed it, that it might be more generally known. It is my best Document. He has given publicity to things that would not have been believed from me. Indeed Some things that I Should never have known without it. The Pamphlet was industriously circulated among his Friends although they were ashamed of it.

BENJAMIN STODDERT TO JOHN ADAMS,
BLADENSBURG, MD., 12 OCTOBER 1809
As to General Hamilton, I scarcely knew him; and perhaps my crime as to him was that, though believing highly of the bril-

liancy of his talents and of his sincere patriotism and honorable principles, I never entertained an exalted opinion of his discretion or the solidity of his judgment, and always thought it unfortunate for the Federal party, and of course for the country,—for I believe the views of that party have always been directed to the best interests of the country, that the opinions of this gentleman were deemed so oracular.

THOMAS JEFFERSON TO JOEL BARLOW, MONTICELLO,
24 JANUARY 1810

The dissensions between two members of the Cabinet are to be lamented. But why should these force Mr. Gallatin to withdraw? They cannot be greater than between Hamilton and myself, and yet we served together four years in that way. We had indeed no personal dissensions. Each of us, perhaps, thought well of the other as a man, but as politicians it was impossible for two men to be of more opposite principles.

ROBERT TROUP: NARRATIVE, ALBANY, N.Y.,
22 MARCH 1810

Whilst at [Kings] College, the General was attentive to public worship; and in the habit of praying upon his knees both night and morning. I lived in the same Room with him for sometime; and I have often been powerfully affected, by the fervor and eloquence of his prayers. The General had read most of the polemical writers on Religious subjects; and he was a zealous believer in the fundamental doctrines of Christianity; and I confess, that the arguments with which he was accustomed to justify his belief, have tended, in no small degree, to confirm my own faith in revealed Religion. When he commanded a company of Artillery in the summer of 1776, I paid him a visit;

and at night, and in the morning, he went to prayer in his usual mode.

THOMAS JEFFERSON TO BENJAMIN RUSH, MONTICELLO, 16 JANUARY 1811

I received a letter from President Washington, then at Mount Vernon, desiring me to call together the Heads of departments, and to invite Mr. Adams to join us in order to determine on some measure which required despatch; and he desired me to act on it, as decided, without again recurring to him. I invited them to dine with me, and after dinner, sitting at our wine, having settled our question, other conversation came on, in which a collision of opinion arose between Mr. Adams and Colonel Hamilton, on the merits of the British constitution, Mr. Adams giving it as his opinion, that, if some of its defects and abuses were corrected, it would be the most perfect constitution of government ever devised by man. Hamilton, on the contrary, asserted, that with its existing vices, it was the most perfect model of government that could be formed; and that the correction of its vices would render it an impracticable government. And this you may be assured was the real line of difference between the political principles of these two gentlemen. Another incident took place on the same occasion, which will further delineate Mr. Hamilton's political principles. The room being hung around with a collection of the portraits of remarkable men, among them were those of Bacon, Newton and Locke, Hamilton asked me who they were. I told him they were my trinity of the three greatest men the world had ever produced, naming them. He paused for some time: "the greatest man," said he, "that ever lived, was Julius Caesar." Mr. Adams was honest as a politician, as well as a man; Hamilton honest as a man, but, as a politician, believing in the necessity of either force or corruption to govern man.

GOUVERNEUR MORRIS TO ROBERT WALSH,
5 FEBRUARY 1811

Speaking of General Hamilton, he had little share in forming the Constitution. He disliked it, believing all republican government to be radically defective. He admired, nevertheless, the British constitution, which I consider as an aristocracy in fact, though a monarchy in name. General Hamilton hated republican government; and he detested the latter, because he believed it must end in despotism, and, be in the mean time, destructive to public morality. He believed that our administration would be enfeebled progressively at every new election, and become at last contemptible. He apprehended that the minions of faction would sell themselves and their country as soon as foreign powers should think it worth while to make the purchase. In short, his study of ancient history impressed on his mind a conviction that democracy, ending in tyranny, is, while it lasts, a cruel and oppressing domination. One marked trait of the General's character was the pertinacious adherence to opinions he had once formed. From his situation in early life, it was not to be expected that he should have a fellow-feeling with those who idly supposed themselves to be the natural aristocracy of this country. In maturer age, his observation and good sense demonstrated that the materials for an aristocracy do not exist in America; wherefore, taking the people as a mass in which there was nothing of family, wealth, prejudice, or habit to raise a permanent mound of distinction. . . .

General Hamilton was of that kind of man which may most safely be trusted; for he was more covetous of glory than of wealth or power. But he was of all men the most indiscreet. He knew that a limited monarchy, even if established, could not preserve itself in this country. He knew, also, that it could not be established, because there is not the regular gradation of ranks among our citizens which is essential to that species of government, and he very well knew that no monarchy whatever could be established but by the mob. When a multitude of indigent, profligate people can be collected and organized, their envy of wealth, talents, and reputation will induce them to give themselves a master, provided that, in so doing, they can mortify and humble their superiors. But there is no instance to prove, and it is, indeed, flatly absurd to suppose, that the upper ranks of society will, by setting up a king, put down themselves. Fortunately for us, no such mass of people can be collected in America. None such exists. But although General Hamilton knew these things, from the study of history, he never failed, on every occasion, to advocate the excellence of and avow his attachment to monarchical government. By this course he not only cut himself off from the views of his opponents, who, with the fondness for wealth and power which he had not, affected a love for the people which he had and which they had not. Thus, meaning very well, he acted very ill, and approached the evils he apprehended by his very solicitude to keep them at a distance.

JAMES MCHENRY TO TIMOTHY PICKERING,
NEAR BALTIMORE, MD., 23 FEBRUARY 1811

Mr. Adams, for reasons best known to himself, endeavors to represent General Hamilton as a man without fair pretensions to sound judgments or useful talents, a visionary politician consumed by indelicate pleasures and a censurable ambition. . . . As to their minds abstractly considered, Hamilton's was profound, penetrating, and invariably sound, and his genius of that rare kind which enlightens the judgment without misleading it; the mind of Mr. Adams, like the last glimmering of a lamp, feeble, wavering, and unsteady, with occasionally a strong flash of light, his genius little, and that little insufficient to irradiate his judgment.

JOHN ADAMS TO BENJAMIN WATERHOUSE, QUINCY, MASS., JULY 12, 1811

If there ever was an "Hamiltonian Conspiracy" as you call it; and as you seem to suppose: I have reason to think its object was not "a Northern Confederation." Hamilton's Ambition was too large for so small an Aim. He aimed at commanding the whole Union, and He did not like to be Shackled even with an Alliance with G. Britain. I know that Pickering was disappointed in not finding Hamilton zealous for an Alliance with England, when We were at Swords Points with France! and I have information, which I believe, but could not legally prove perhaps, that Pickering was mortified to find that neither Hamilton nor King would adopt the Plan that he carried from Boston, in his Way to Congress after he was first chosen into the Senate, of a division of the States and a Northern Confederacy. No! H. had wider Views! If he could have made a Tool of Adams as he did of Washington, he hoped to erect such a Government as he pleased over the whole Union, and enter into Alliance with France or England as would suit his Convenience.

H. and Burr, in point of Ambition were equal. In Principle equal. In Talents different: H. superiour in Literary Talents: B. in military. H. a Nevis Adventurer. B. descended from the earliest, most learned Pious and virtuous of our American Nation, and buoyed up by the Prejudices of half the Nation. He found himself thwarted, persecuted, calumniated by a wandering Stranger. The deep Malice of H. against Burr, and his indefatigable Exertions to defame him are little known. I know so much of it for a Course of years, that I wondered a Duel had not taken Place Seven Years before it did. I could have produced such a Duel at any Moment for Seven Years. I kept the Secrets Sacred and inviolable: and have kept it them to this day.

JOHN ADAMS TO BENJAMIN RUSH, QUINCY, MASS., 28 AUGUST 1811

If I should inculcate fidelity to the marriage bed, it would be said, that it proceeded from resentment to General Hamilton and a malicious desire to hold up to posterity his libertinism.

JOHN ADAMS TO THE PRINTERS OF THE BOSTON PATRIOT, JUNE 1812

The Truth is, that Hamilton's soul was corroded by that mordant sublimated Spirit of Ambition, that subjugates every Thing to its own Interest; and considers every Man of superior Age and merit, or who had the reputation of superior merit, as its Enemy.

JOHN ADAMS TO THE PRINTERS OF THE BOSTON PATRIOT, JUNE 1812

But it seems my "Personal Friends" "disparaged" his "motives" from another Topic, namely by calling him a "Factious Spirit," a "versatile Spirit," who could not be long satisfied with any Chief however meritorious.

Really, if I should believe this to be true, I must take Mr. Hamilton's Word for it. I never knew that I had such "personal Friends." I never knew that I had any Friends who had so much sagacity as to penetrate this Truth, or so much fortitude as to declare it. I will say nothing of the "factious Spirit." Let Posterity judge. Let the World judge. But "a versatile Spirit" he cannot be called, unless in an hypocritical sense. His invariable object was the head of this Nation, whether as President, as Monarch, or as Despot with an Army of Conscripts at his heels. "Empire! Empire! Empire! Let that Word make sacred all I do or can attempt." This was his whole creed, theological, philosophical, moral, political and civil. From this Principle, which in my opinion was his only Principle, he scorned and defamed Washington, whenever Washington would not be his Tool, from this Principle he calumniated Burr, with a cool deliberate, insidious, persevering malice, the parallel of which I never knew, and which finally cost him his life. From this Principle, he libeled Adams. From this Principle he calumniated every Man who stood before him, every Man who stood on equal ground with him, and every Man who was after him near enough, to have a probability or possibility of coming up with him. From this Principle he gave the go by to Mr. Jay, by propagating the Idea that he was a "degraded Character" and became a religious "Fanatick." He could not surely be called "a versatile Spirit." My "personal Friends were in an error; quite mistaken, if they called him a "versatile Spirit." His object was invariable, not versatile, viz. Supreme Power; his means were invariably the same, viz. Libels, lies and slanders, therefore certainly not versatile.

JOHN ADAMS TO THE PRINTERS OF THE *BOSTON PATRIOT*, JUNE 1812

This was so precisely the Character of Hamilton, that every Man above him, every man on a line with him, and every man below him, who could be suspected by him of a possibility of a competition with him for the highest Power, was sure to be blasphemed blasted and persecuted by himself and his Friends.

JOHN ADAMS TO THE PRINTERS OF THE *BOSTON PATRIOT*, JUNE 1812

Hamilton had no more gratitude than a Cat. If you give a hungry famished Cat a slice of meat, she will not accept it as a Gift; she will snatch at it by Force, and express in her countenance and air, that she is under no obligation to you; that she got it by her own cunning and activity, and that you are a fool for giving it to her.

JOHN ADAMS TO THE PRINTERS OF THE BOSTON PATRIOT, JUNE 1812
... this West Indian Boy just from Scotland ....

JOHN ADAMS TO THE PRINTERS OF THE BOSTON PATRIOT, JUNE 1812
After the War broke out this Scotch Creolian Boy crept into the Army as a something, I know not what, whether a volunteer, an ensign, an Aide de Camp, a scribbler or a Secretary, or a Colonel I neither know nor care, as an Adventurer, a hungry wolf who had no other way to subsist himself or prowl for prey I believe.

JOHN ADAMS TO THOMAS JEFFERSON, QUINCY, MASS., 12 JULY 1813
... a bastard Bratt of a Scotch Pedlar. ...

JOHN ADAMS TO THOMAS JEFFERSON, QUINCY, MASS., 3 SEPTEMBER 1816
The Death of Hamilton, under all its circumstances, produced a General Grief. His most determined Enemies did not like to get rid of him, in that Way. They pitied too his Widow and Children. His Party seized the moment of public Feeling to come forward with Funeral Orations and Printed Panegyricks reinforced with mock Funerals and solemn Grimaces, and all this by People who have buried Otis, Sam. Adams, Hancock and Gerry in Comparative Obscurity.

Hamilton was indeed a singular character. Of acute understanding, disinterested, honest, and honorable in all private transactions, amiable in society, and duly valuing virtue in private life, yet so bewitched & perverted by the British example, as to be under thorough conviction that corruption was essential to the government of a nation.

JOHN ADAMS TO THOMAS JEFFERSON, QUINCY, MASS.,
21 DECEMBER 1819
The Missouri question I hope will follow the other Waves under the Ship and do no harm. I know it is high treason to express a doubt of the perpetual duration of our vast American Empire, and our free Institutions, and I say as devoutly as Father Paul, esto perpetua [be thou everlasting], but I am sometimes Cassandra enough to dream that another Hamilton, another Burr might rend this mighty Fabric in twain, or perhaps into a leash, and a few more choice Spirits of the same Stamp, might produce as many Nations in North America as there are in Europe.

JOHN ADAMS TO THOMAS JEFFERSON, QUINCY, MASS.,
15 OCTOBER 1822
Hamilton's hobby was the Army.

JAMES KENT TO MRS. ELIZABETH HAMILTON, NEW YORK,
10 DECEMBER 1832
I knew General Hamilton's character well. His life and actions, for the course of twenty-two years, had engaged and fixed my attention. They were often passing under my eye and observation. For the last six years of his life he was arguing causes before me. I have been sensibly struck, in a thousand instances, with his habitual reverence for truth, his candor, his ardent attachment to civil liberty, his indignation at oppression of every kind, his abhorrence of every semblance of fraud, his

reverence for justice, and his sound legal principles drawn by a clear and logical deduction from the purest Christian ethics, and from the very foundations of all rational and practical jurisprudence. He was blessed with a very amiable, generous, tender, and charitable disposition, and he had the most artless simplicity of any man I ever knew. It was impossible not to love as well as respect and admire him. He was perfectly disinterested. The selfish principle, that infirmity too often of great as well as of little minds, seemed never to have reached him. It was entirely incompatible with the purity of his taste and the grandeur of his ambition. Everything appeared to be at once extinguished, when it came in competition with his devotion to his country's welfare and glory. He was a most faithful friend to the cause of civil liberty throughout the world, but he was a still greater friend to truth and justice.

JAMES KENT JOURNAL, 1833

[Egbert Benson] says when Gen. Washington came on to assume the Government in 1789 he asked Robert Morris *what was to be done with the national Debt,* & Mr. Morris replied that he was glad the subject was mentioned, since he could not undertake the Office of Financier if it was offered to him, & that there was but one man who was competent to answer the question that man was *Alexander Hamilton.*

Hamilton's Descriptions of Others

JOHN ADAMS

TO THEODORE SEDGWICK, NEW YORK, 9 OCTOBER 1788
On the subject of Vice President, my ideas have concurred with your, and I believe Mr. Adams will have the votes of this state. He will certainly, I think, be preferred to the other Gentleman [John Hancock]. Yet, *certainly,* is perhaps too strong a word. I can conceive that the other, who is supposed to be a more pliable man may command Antifoederal influence.

The only hesitation in my mind with regard to Mr. Adams has arisen within a day or two; from a suggestion by a particular Gentleman that he is unfriendly in his sentiments to General Washington. Richard H. Lee who will probably, as rumor now runs, come from Virginia [to the U.S. Senate] is also in this state [i.e., of opposing Washington]. The Lees and Adams' have been in the habit of uniting; and hence may spring up a Cabal very embarrassing to the Executive and of course to the administration of the Government. Consider this. Sound the reality of it and let me hear from you.

TO JAMES MADISON, NEW YORK, 23 NOVEMBER 1788
On the whole I have concluded to support Adams [for Vice President]; though I am not without apprehensions on the score we have conversed about. My principal reasons are these—First He is a declared partisan of referring to future experience the expediency of amendments in the system (and though I do not *altogether* adopt this sentiment) it is much nearer my own than certain other doctrines. Secondly a character of importance in the Eastern states, if he is not Vice President, one of two worse things will be likely to happen— Either he must be nominated to some important office for which he is less proper, or will become a malcontent and pos-

sibly espouse and give additional weight to the opposition to the Government.

TO CHARLES COTESWORTH PINCKNEY, PHILADELPHIA,
10 OCTOBER 1792
Mr. Adams, whatever objections may be against some of his theoretic opinions, is a firm honest independent politician.

TO JOHN STEELE, PHILADELPHIA, 15 OCTOBER 1792
Mr. Adams like other men has his faults and his foibles. Some of the opinions he is supposed to entertain, we do not approve—but we believe him to be honest firm faithful and independent—a sincere lover of his country—a real friend to genuine liberty; but combining his attachment to that with the love of order and stable government. No man's private character can be fairer than his. No man has given stronger proofs than him of disinterested & intrepid patriotism.

TO RUFUS KING, NEW YORK, 5 JANUARY 1800
At home, every thing is in the main well; except as to the Perverseness and capriciousness of one [Adams] and the spirit of faction of many.

TO JAMES MCHENRY, NEW YORK, 6 JUNE 1800
The man is more mad than I ever thought him and I shall soon be led to say as wicked as he is mad.

TO CHARLES CARROLL OF CARROLLTON, NEW YORK,
1 JULY 1800
On this point there is some danger, though the greatest number of strong minded men in New England are not only satisfied of the expediency of supporting [Thomas] *Pinckney,* as giving the best chance against Jefferson, but even prefer him

to *Adams*; yet in the body of the people there is a strong personal attachment to this gentleman, and most of the leaders of the second class are so anxious for his re-election that it will be difficult to convince them that there is as much danger of its failure as there unquestionably is, or to induce them faithfully to cooperate in Mr. Pinckney, notwithstanding their common and strong dread of Jefferson. . . .

That this gentleman ought not to be the object of the federal wish, is, with me, reduced to demonstration. His administration has already very materially disgraced and sunk the government. There are defects in his character which must inevitably continue to do this more and more. And if he is supported by the federal party, his party must in the issue fall with him. Every other calculation will, in my judgment, prove illusory.

Doctor *Franklin*, a sagacious observer of human nature, drew this portrait of Mr. Adams:—"He is always honest, *sometimes* great, but *often mad.*" I subscribe to the justness of this picture, adding as to the first trait of it this qualification—"as far as a man excessively *vain* and *jealous,* and *ignobly* attached to *place* can be."

TO CHARLES CARROLL OF CARROLLTON, NEW YORK, 7 AUGUST 1800

As between [Thomas] Pinckney & Adams I give a decided preference to the first. If you have not heard enough to induce you to agree in this opinion I will upon your request enter into my reasons. Mr. Adams has governed & must govern from *impulse* and *caprice,* under the influence of the two most mischievous of Passions for a Politician, to an extreme that to be portrayed would present a caricature—*Vanity* and *Jealousy*. He has already disorganized & in a great measure prostrated the Federal Party.

LETTER CONCERNING THE PUBLIC CONDUCT AND CHARACTER OF JOHN ADAMS, NEW YORK, 24 OCTOBER 1800

He has certain fixed points of character which tend naturally to the detriment of any cause of which he is the chief, of any administration of which he is the head; that by his ill humors and jealousies he has already divided and distracted the supporters of the government; that he has furnished deadly weapons to its enemies by unfounded accusations, and has weakened the force of its friends by decrying some of the most influential of them to the utmost of his power.

LETTER CONCERNING THE PUBLIC CONDUCT AND CHARACTER OF JOHN ADAMS, NEW YORK, 24 OCTOBER 1800

Few go as far in their objections [to the reelection of Adams as President] as I do. Not denying to Mr. Adams patriotism and integrity, and even talents of a certain kind, I should be deficient in candor, were I to conceal the conviction, that he does not possess the talents adapted to the *Administration* of Government, and that there are great and intrinsic defects in his character, which unfit him for the office of Chief Magistrate. . . .

I was one of that numerous class who had conceived a high veneration for Mr. Adams, on account of the part he acted in the first stages of our revolution. My imagination had exalted him to a high eminence, as a man of patriotic, bold, profound, and comprehensive mind. But in the progress of the war, opinions were ascribed to him, which brought into question, with me, the solidity of his understanding. . . . I remember also, that they had the effect of inducing me to qualify the admiration which I had once entertained for him, and to reserve for opportunities of future scrutiny, a definitive opinion of the true standard of his character. . . .

But this did not hinder me from making careful observations upon his several communications, and endeavoring to derive from them an accurate idea of his talents and character. This scrutiny enhanced my esteem in the main for his moral qualifications, but lessened my respect for his intellectual endowments. I then adopted an opinion, which all my subsequent experience has confirmed, that he is a man of an imagination sublimated and eccentric; propitious neither to the regular display of sound judgment, nor to steady perseverance in a systematic plan of conduct; and I began to perceive what has been since too manifest, that to this defect are added the unfortunate foibles of a vanity without bounds, and a jealousy capable of discoloring every object. . . .

The particulars of this Journal [i.e., Adams's diary entrees while a peace commissioner] cannot be expected to have remained in my memory—but I recollect one which may serve as a sample. Being among the guests invited to dine with the Count de Vergennes, Minister for Foreign Affairs, Mr. Adams thought fit to give a specimen of American politeness, by conducting Madame de Vergennes to dinner; in the way, she was pleased to make retribution in the current coin of French politeness—by saying to him, *"Monsieur Adams, vous etes le* Washington *de negotiation."* Stating the incident, he makes this comment upon it: "These people have a very pretty knack of paying compliments." He might have added, they have also a very dexterous knack of disguising a sarcasm. . . .

A primary cause of the state of things which led to this event, is to be traced to the ungovernable temper of Mr. Adams. It is a fact that he is often liable to paroxysms of anger, which deprive him of self command, and produce very outrageous behavior to those who approach him. Most, if not all his Ministers, and several distinguished Members of the two Houses of Congress, have been humiliated by the effects of these gusts of passion."

JACOB ADGATE AND MATHEW FORD

TO ROBERT LIVINGSTON, 25 APRIL 1785
The truth is that the state is now governed by a couple of New England adventurers—Ford and Adgate; who make tools of the Yates* and their Associates. A number of attempts have been made by this junto to subvert the constitution and destroy the rights of private property; which but for the Council of Revision would have had the most serious effects.
*Abraham and Robert Yates.

ROBERT BARNWELL

TO EDWARD CARRINGTON, PHILADELPHIA, 26 MAY 1792
Mr. Barnwell of South Carolina . . . appears to be a man of nice honor.

CHARLES BIDDLE

TO PRESIDENT GEORGE WASHINGTON, PHILADELPHIA, 14 JUNE 1794
Mr. Biddle has many things in his favor. Perhaps he has more ability than any of the persons named [as candidates for Supervisor of Pennsylvania], and no doubts are entertained of his firmness, activity or attention. His connections and influence are principally among the malcontents. But most persons who have been consulted entertain an unfavorable impression of his political principles, & think there is not full assurance that he would not sacrifice the duties of his station & the interests of the Government to party considerations. He was named by the *Democratic Society* vice President, which he has it seems neither accepted nor publicly disavowed. Several attach an idea of cunning & duplicity to the character. *One* good

judge of characters thinks favorably of his principles & that reliance may be placed. But the result of a comprehensive enquiry is that there would be hazard in the appointment and the case is believed to be one in which nothing ought to be hazarded.

THEODORICK BLAND

TO ROBERT HANSON HARRISON, PHILADELPHIA,
27 OCTOBER 1780
Bland is very clever & without question wishes to push on in the true & right road [supporting Washington and the army].

AARON BURR

TO HUGH SETON, NEW YORK, 1 JANUARY 1785
Mr. Burr who is a member of the Assembly, of influence and abilities. . . .

FROM ALEXANDER HAMILTON, PHILADELPHIA,
21 SEPTEMBER 1792
Mr. Clinton's success [in winning the vice presidency] I should think very unfortunate. I am not for trusting the Government too much in the hands of its enemies. But still Mr. C——— is a man of property, and, in private life, as far as I know of probity. I fear the other Gentleman is unprincipled both as a public and private man. When the constitution was in deliberation, his conduct was equivocal; but its enemies, who I believe best understood him considered him as with them. In fact, I take it, he is for or against nothing, but as it suits his interest or ambition. He is determined, as I conceive, to make his way to be the head of the popular party and to climb per

fas et nefas* to the highest honors of the state; and as much higher as circumstances may permit. Embarrassed, as I understand, in his circumstances, with an extravagant family—bold enterprising and intriguing, I am mistaken, if it be not his object to play the game of confusion, and I feel it a religious duty to oppose his career.

*Legally or illegally.

FROM ALEXANDER HAMILTON, PHILADELPHIA, 26 SEPTEMBER 1792

Mr. Burr's integrity as an Individual is not unimpeached. As a public man he is one of the worst sort—a friend to nothing but as it suits his interest and ambition. Determined to climb to the highest honours of State, and as much higher as circumstances may permit—he cares nothing about the means of effecting his purpose. Tis evident that he aims at putting himself at the head of what he calls the "popular party" as affording the best tools for an ambitious man to work with. Secretly turning Liberty into ridicule he, knows as well as most men how to make use of the name. In a word, if we have an embryo-Caesar in the United States 'tis Burr.

TO CHARLES COTESWORTH PINCKNEY, PHILADELPHIA, 10 OCTOBER 1792

[Burr] has no other principle than to *mount at all events* to the first honors of the State & to as much more as circumstances will permit—a man in private life not unblemished.

TO JOHN STEELE, PHILADELPHIA, 15 OCTOBER 1792

My opinion of Mr. Burr is yet to form—but according to the present state of it, he is a man whose only political principle is, to *mount at all events* to the highest legal honors of the

Nation and as much further as circumstances will carry him. Imputations not favorable to his integrity as a man rest upon him; but I do not vouch for their authenticity.

TO OLIVER WOLCOTT, JR., NEW YORK, 28 JUNE 1798
Col. Burr sets out today for Philadelphia. I have some reasons for wishing that the administration may manifest a cordiality to him. It is not impossible he will be found a useful cooperator. I am aware there are different sides but the case is worth the experiment. He will call on McHenry upon going to the City.

TO JAMES A. BAYARD, NEW YORK, 6 AUGUST 1800
There seems to be too much probability that Jefferson or Burr will be President. The latter is intriguing with all his might in New Jersey, Rhode-Island & Vermont. And there is a possibility of some success to his intrigues. He counts positively on the universal support of the Antis: & that by some adventitious aid from other quarters, he will overtop his friend Jefferson. Admitting the first point the conclusion may be realized. And if it is Burr will certainly attempt to reform the Government *a la Buonaparte.* He is as unprincipled & dangerous a man as any country can boast; as true a *Cataline* as ever met in midnight conclave.

TO OLIVER WOLCOTT, JR., NEW YORK, 16 DECEMBER 1800
It is now, my Dear Sir, ascertained that Jefferson or Burr will be President and it seems probable that they will come with equal votes to the House of Representatives. It is also circulated here that in this event the Federalists in Congress or some of them talk of preferring Burr. I trust New England at least will not so far lose its head as to fall into this snare. There is no doubt but that upon every virtuous and prudent calcu-

lation Jefferson is to be preferred. He is by far not so dangerous a man and he has pretensions to character.

As to *Burr* there is nothing in his favour. His private character is not defended by his most partial friends. He is bankrupt beyond redemption except by the plunder of his country. His public principles have no other spring or aim than his own aggrandizement per *fas* et *nefas*.* If he can, he will certainly disturb our institutions to secure to himself *permanent power* and with it *wealth*. He is truly the *Cataline* of America—& if I may credit Major Wilcocks, he has held very vindictive language respecting his opponents.

But early measures must be taken to fix on this point the opinions of the Federalists. Among them, from different motives—Burr will find partisans. If the thing be neglected he may possibly go far.

Yet it may be well enough to throw out a lure for him, in order to tempt him to start for the plate & thus lay the foundation of dissention between the two chiefs.

*Legally or illegally.

TO THEODORE SEDGWICK, NEW YORK, 22 DECEMBER 1800
The appointment of Burr, as President would disgrace our Country abroad. No agreement with him [and Federalists] could be relied upon. His private circumstances render disorder a necessary resource. His public principles offer no obstacle. His ambition aims at nothing short of permanent power and wealth in his own person. For heaven's sake let not the Federal party be responsible for the elevation of this Man.

TO HARRISON GRAY OTIS, NEW YORK, 23 DECEMBER 1800
Burr loves nothing but himself; thinks of nothing but his own aggrandizement, and will be content with nothing, short of

permanent power in his own hands. No compact that he should make with any passion in his breast, except ambition, could be relied upon by himself. How then should we be able to rely upon any agreement with him. Jefferson, I suspect, will not dare much. Burr will dare every thing, in the sanguine hope of effecting every thing.

TO GOUVERNEUR MORRIS, NEW YORK, 24 DECEMBER 1800
Another subject—*Jefferson* or *Burr*?—the former without all doubt. The latter in my judgment has no principle public or private—could be bound by no agreement—will listen to no monitor but his ambition; & for this purpose will use the *worst* part of the community as a ladder to climb to permanent power & an instrument to crush the better part. He is bankrupt beyond redemption except by the resources that grow out of war and disorder or by a sale to a foreign power or by great peculation. War with Great Britain would be the immediate instrument. He is sanguine enough to hope every thing—daring enough to attempt every thing—wicked enough to scruple nothing. From the elevation of such a man heaven preserve the Country!

TO GOUVERNEUR MORRIS, NEW YORK, 26 DECEMBER 1800
That the Convention with France ought to be ratified as the least of two evils. That on the same ground Jefferson ought to be preferred to Burr. I trust the Federalists will not finally be so mad as to vote for the latter. I speak with an intimate & accurate knowledge of character. His elevation can only promote the purposes of the desperate and profligate. If there be a man in the world I ought to hate it is Jefferson. With Burr I have always been personally well. But the public good must be paramount to every private consideration. My opinion may be freely used with such reserves as you shall think discreet.

TO JAMES A. BAYARD, NEW YORK, 27 DECEMBER 1800

Several letters to myself & others from the City of Washington, excite in my mind extreme alarm on the subject of the future President. It seems nearly ascertained that *Jefferson & Burr* will come into the House of Representatives with equal votes, and those letters express the probability that the Federal Party may prefer the latter. In my opinion a circumstance more ruinous to them, or more disastrous to the Country could not happen. This opinion is dictated by a long & close attention to the character, with the best opportunities of knowing it; an advantage for judging which few of our friends possess, & which ought to give some weight to my opinion. Be assured my dear Sir, that this man has no principle public or private. As a politician his sole spring of action is an inordinate ambition; as an individual he is believed by friends as well as foes to be without *probity*, and a voluptuary by system, with habits of expense that can be satisfied by no fair expedients. As to his talents, great management & cunning are the predominant features—he is yet to give proofs of those solid abilities which characterize the statesman. Daring & energy must be allowed him but these qualities under the direction of the worst passions, are certainly strong objections not recommendations. He is of a temper to undertake the most hazardous enterprises because he is sanguine enough to think nothing impracticable, and of an ambition which will be content with nothing less than *permanent* power in his own hands. The maintenance of the existing institutions will not suit him, because under them his power will be too narrow & too precarious; yet the innovations he may attempt will not offer the substitute of a system *durable* & *safe,* calculated to give lasting prosperity, & to unite liberty with strength. It will be the system of the day, sufficient to serve his own turn, & not looking beyond himself. To execute this plan as the good men of the country cannot be relied upon, the worst will be used. Let it not be imagined that the difficulties of execution will deter, or a calculation of interest restrain. The truth is that under forms of Government like ours, too much is practicable to men who will without scruple avail themselves of the bad passions of human nature. To a man of this description possessing the requisite talents, the acquisition of permanent power is not a Chimera. I *know* that Mr. Burr does not view it as such, & I am sure there are no means too atrocious to be employed by him. In debt vastly beyond his means of payment, with all the habits of excessive expense, he cannot be satisfied with the regular emoluments of any office of our Government. Corrupt expedients will be to him a *necessary* resource. Will any prudent man offer such a president to the temptations of foreign gold? No engagement that can be made with him can be depended upon. While making it he will laugh in his sleeve at the credulity of those with whom he makes it—and the first moment it suits his views to break it he will do so. Let me add that I could scarcely name a discreet man of either party in our State, who does not think Mr. Burr the most unfit man in the U.S. for the office of President. Disgrace abroad [&] ruin at home are the probable fruits of his elevation. To contribute to the disappointment and mortification of Mr. J[efferson] would be on my part, only to retaliate for unequivocal proofs of enmity; but in a case like this it would be base to listen to personal considerations. In alluding to the situation I mean only to illustrate how strong must be the motives which induce me to promote *his* elevation in exclusion of another. For Heaven's sake my dear Sir, exert yourself to the utmost to save our country from so great a calamity. Let us not be responsible for the evils which in all probability will follow the preference. All calculations that may lead to it must prove fallacious.

TO JAMES ROSS, NEW YORK, 29 DECEMBER 1800

Letters which myself and others have received from Washington give me much alarm at the prospect that Mr. Burr may be supported by the Federalists in preference to Mr. Jefferson. Be assured, my Dear Sir, that this would be a fatal mistake. From a thorough knowledge of the character I can pronounce with confidence that Mr. Burr is the last man in the United States to be supported by the Federalists.

1. It is an opinion firmly entertained by his enemies and not disputed by his friends that as a man he is deficient in *honesty*. Some very sad stories are related of him. That he is bankrupt for a large *deficit* is certain.

2. As a politician discerning men of both parties admit that he has but one principle—to *get power* by *any* means and to *keep* it by *all* means.

3. Of an ambition too irregular and inordinate to be content with institutions that leave his power precarious, he is of too bold and sanguine a temper to think anything too hazardous to be attempted or too difficult to be accomplished.

4. As to talents they are great for management and intrigue—but he is yet to give the first proofs that they are equal to the art of governing well.

5. As to his theory, no mortal can tell what it is. Institutions that would serve his own purpose (such as the Government of France of the present day) not such as would promote lasting prosperity and glory to the Country would be his preference because he cares only for himself and nothing for his Country or glory.

6. Certain that his irregular ambition cannot be supported by *good* men, he will *court* and *employ* the worst men

of all parties as the most eligible instruments. Jacobinism in its most pernicious form will scourge the country.

7. As to foreign policies, War will be a necessary mean of power and wealth. The animosity to the British will be the handle by which he will attempt to wield the nation to that point: Within a fortnight he has advocated positions which if acted upon would in six months place us in a state of War with that power.

From the Elevation of such a man may heaven preserve the Country. Should it be by the means of the Federalists I should at once despair. I should see no longer anything upon which to rest the hope of public or private prosperity.

TO JAMES MCHENRY, NEW YORK, 4 JANUARY 1801
Nothing has given me so much chagrin as the Intelligence that the Federal Party were thinking seriously of supporting Mr. Burr for President. I should consider the execution of the plan as devoting the country and signing their own death warrant. Mr. Burr will probably make stipulations, but he will laugh in his sleeve while he makes them and he will break them the first moment it may serve his purpose. But will not his interest govern him? It doubtless will, as he understands it. But *stable* power and great *wealth* being his objects, and these being unattainable by means that the sober part of the Federalists will countenance, he will certainly deceive and disappoint them. A H____ Lee* &c. &c. may find their account in it but good men in the Country never will. At least such ought to be the calculation; from a profligate, a bankrupt, a man who laughing at democracy has played the whole game of Jacobinism nothing better ought to be expected. Nor should a mere chapter

of accidents be hazarded; it ought to be enough for us to know that he is certainly one of the most unprincipled men in the United States.

*Henry Lee, the former governor of Virginia supported Burr's election over Jefferson in the U.S. House of Representatives.

TO JAMES A. BAYARD, NEW YORK, 16 JANUARY 1801

As to Burr these things are admitted and indeed cannot be denied, that he is a man of *extreme & irregular* ambition—that he is *selfish* to a degree which excludes all social affections & that he is decidedly *profligate*. But it is said, 1st. that he is *artful & dexterous* to accomplish his ends—2nd. that he holds no pernicious theories, but is a mere *matter of fact* man—3rd. that his very selfishness is a guard against mischievous foreign predilections. 4th That his *local situation* has enabled him to appreciate the utility of our Commercial & fiscal systems, and the same quality of selfishness will lead him to support & invigorate them. 5th. that he is now disliked by the Jacobins [i.e., Jeffersonians], that his elevation will be a mortal stab to them, breed an invincible hatred to him, & compel him to lean on the Federalists. 6th. That Burr's ambition will be checked by his good sense, by the manifest impossibility of succeeding in any scheme of usurpation, & that if attempted, there is nothing to fear from the attempt. These topics are in my judgment more plausible than solid. As to the 1st point the fact must be admitted, but those qualities are objections rather than recommendations when they are under the direction of bad principles. As to the 2nd point too much is taken for granted. If Burr's conversation is to be credited he is not very far from being a visionary. It is ascertained in some instances that he has talked perfect *Godwinism*.* I have myself heard him speak with applause of the French system as unshackling the mind & leaving it to its natural energies, and I have been present when he has contended against Banking Systems with earnestness & with the same arguments that Jefferson would use. The truth is that *Burr* is a man of a very subtle imagination, and a mind of this make is rarely free from ingenious whimsies. Yet I admit that he has no fixed theory & that his peculiar notions will easily give way to his interest. But is it a recommendation to have *no theory?* Can that man be a systematic or able statesman who has none? I believe not. *No general principles* will hardly work much better than erroneous ones. As to the 3rd. point—it is certain that Burr generally speaking has been as warm a partisan of France as Jefferson—that he has in some instances shown himself to be so with passion. But if it was from calculation who will say that his calculations will not continue him so? His selfishness so far from being an obstacle may be a prompter. If corrupt as well as selfish he may be a partisan for gain—if ambitious as well as selfish, he may be a partisan for the sake of aid to his views. No man has trafficked more than he in the floating passions of the multitude. Hatred to G. Britain & attachment to France in the public mind will naturally lead a man of his selfishness, attached to place and power, to favor France & oppose G. Britain. The Gallicism of many of our patriots is to be thus resolved, & in my opinion it is morally certain that Burr will continue to be influenced by this calculation. As to the 4th point the instance I have cited with respect to Banks proves that the argument is not to be relied on. If there was much in it, why does Chancellor [Robert R.] Livingston maintain that we ought not to cultivate navigation but ought to let foreigners be our carriers? France is of this opinion too & Burr for some reason or other, will be very apt to be of the opinion of *France*. As to the 5th point—nothing can be more fallacious. It is demonstrated by recent facts that Burr is *solicitous* to *keep* upon *Antifederal ground,* to avoid compromising himself by any engagements with the Federalists. With or without such engagements he will easily persuade his former friends that he does stand on that ground, & after their first resentment they will be glad to rally under him. In the mean time he will take care not to disoblige them & he will always court those among them who are best fitted for tools. He will never choose to lean on good men because he knows that they will never support his bad projects; but instead of this he will endeavor to disorganize both parties & to form out of them a third composed of men fitted by their characters to be conspirators, & instruments of such projects. That this will be his future conduct may be inferred from his past plan, & from the admitted quality of irregular ambition. Let it be remembered that Mr. Burr has never appeared solicitous for fame, & that great Ambition unchecked by principle, or the love of Glory, is an unruly Tyrant which never can keep long in a course which good men will approve. As to the last point—The proposition is against the experience of all times. Ambition without principle never was long under the guidance of good sense. Besides that, really the force of Mr. Burr's understanding is much overrated. He is far more *cunning* than *wise*, far more *dexterous* than *able*. In my opinion he is inferior in real ability to Jefferson. There are also facts against the supposition. It is past all doubt that he has blamed me for not having improved the situation I once was in to change the Government. That when answered that this could not have been done without guilt—he replied—"Les grands ames se soucient peu des petits morceaux"**—that when told the thing was never practicable from the genius and situation of the country, he answered, "that depends on the estimate we form of the human passions and of the means of influencing them." Does this prove that Mr. Burr would consider a scheme of usurpation as visionary. The truth is with great apparent coldness he is the most sanguine man in the world. He thinks every thing possible to adventure and perseverance. And though I believe he will fail, I think it almost certain he will attempt usurpation. And the attempt will involve great mischief.

*William Godwin (1756–1836), an English philosopher and novelist who advocated a doctrine of extreme individualism and an anarchistic system of government based upon the goodness of human reasoning.
**Great souls don't worry much about small matters.

WILLIAM PLUMER: MEMORANDUM, 22 JUNE 1807
Alexander Hamilton, who fell by his shot, once said to an acquaintance of mine *(Jona. Mason, Esq.)* "The talents of Mr. Burr are over-rated—the world will ere long know it—His arguments at the bar were concise—his address was pleasing, his manners were more, they were fascinating. When I analyzed his arguments I could not discover in what his greatness consisted. But his ambition is unlimited." Mr. Mason stated these observations of Hamilton to me this day.

MATTHEW CLARKSON

TO PRESIDENT GEORGE WASHINGTON, PHILADELPHIA, 14 JUNE 1794
Mr. Clarkson has several things in favor [of his appointment as supervisor of Pennsylvania], perhaps rather more ability than most of the other persons. But he wants [i.e., needs] bodily activity, which may be a point of consequence & he is said to be much embarrassed in his circumstances.

GEORGE CLINTON

TO ISRAEL PUTNAM, CORYELL'S FERRY, N.J., 30 JULY 1777
General Clinton informs His Excellency [George Washington], that he is called to attend at Kingston and take the oath of office conformable to his appointment as Governor of the

State of New York. It is to be regretted that so useful an officer is obliged to leave the posts under his superintendency at a time like this.

TO ROBERT R. LIVINGSTON, HEADQUARTERS NEAR GERMANTOWN, PA., 7 AUGUST 1777

In a Conversation I lately had with Mr. Jay he mentioned sending Governor Clinton with all the New York Militia of the upper part of your State to assist in opposing Mr. Burgoyne. I wish you may do this of all things. General Clinton is an excellent officer, the people have Confidence in him, will once act with zeal and Serve with Spirit & perseverance under him; his being wanted in the Civil line should be no Objection. It imports you more to take measures for preserving your State than for Governing what you may not long have to Govern. Governor Clinton I am persuaded can render you the most Essential Services in the way proposed.

TO SUSANNA LIVINGSTON, MIDDLEBROOK, N.J., 18 MARCH 1779

I shall therefore only tell you, that whether the governor [Clinton] & the general [George Washington] are more honest, or more perverse, than other people, they have a very odd knack of thinking alike; and it happens in the present case, that they both equally disapprove the intercourse [of people back and forth into British-held territory].

TO ROBERT MORRIS, ALBANY, N.Y., 13 AUGUST 1782

There is no man in the government [of the state of New York] who has a decided influence in it. The present governor has declined in popularity, partly from a defect of qualifications for his station and partly from causes that do him honor—the vigorous execution of some necessary laws that bore hard upon the people, and severity of discipline among the militia. He is, I believe, a man of integrity and passes with his particular friends for a statesman; it is certain that without being destitute of understanding, his passions are much warmer, than his judgment is enlightened. The preservation of his place is an object to his private fortune as well as to his ambition; and we are not to be surprised, if instead of taking a lead in measures that contradict a prevailing prejudice, however he may be convinced of their utility, he either flatters it or temporises; especially when a new election approaches.

TO JAMES MADISON, NEW YORK, 19 MAY 1788
As Clinton is truly the leader of his party, and is inflexibly obstinate I count little on overcoming opposition [to the Constitution] by reason.

TO GOUVERNEUR MORRIS, NEW YORK, 19 MAY 1788
In this state, as far as we can judge, the elections [for the state ratifying convention] have gone wrong. The event however will not certainly be known till the end of the month. Violence rather than moderation is to be looked for from the opposite party. Obstinacy seems the prevailing trait in the character of its leader. The language is, that if all the other states adopt, this is to persist in refusing the Constitution. It is reduced to a certainty that Clinton has in several conversations declared the UNION unnecessary; though I have the information through channels which do not permit a public use to be made of it.

TO JAMES MADISON, POUGHKEEPSIE, N.Y., 2 JULY 1788
[On the debates in the New York ratifying convention.] Our arguments confound, but do not convince. Some of the leaders however appear to me to be convinced *by circumstances* and to

be desirous of a retreat. This does not apply to the Chief, who wishes to establish *Clintonism* on the basis of *Antifederalism*.

H. G. LETTERS NO. 1, NEW YORK *DAILY ADVERTISER*,
10 MARCH 1789

The present Governor was bred to the law, under William Smith, Esquire, formerly of this city. Some time before the late revolution, he resided in Ulster county, and there followed his profession with reputation, though not with distinction. He was not supposed to possess considerable talents; but upon the whole, stood fair on the score of probity. It must however be confessed, that he early got the character with many of being a very *artful* man; and it is not to be wondered at, if that impression, on the minds in which it prevailed, deducted something from the opinion of his integrity. But it would be refining too much to admit such a consequence to be a just one. There are certainly characters (tho' they may be rare) which unite a great degree of address, and even a large portion of what is best expressed by the word CUNNING, with a pretty exact adherence, in the main, to the principles of integrity.

Mr. Clinton, from his youth upwards, has been remarkable for a quality, which, when accompanied by a sound and enlarged understanding, a liberal mind, and a good heart, is denominated *firmness,* and answers the most valuable purposes; but which when joined with narrow views, a prejudiced and contracted disposition, a passionate and interested temper, passes under the name of *obstinacy,* and is a source of the greatest mischiefs, especially in exalted public stations.

H. G. LETTERS NO. 4, NEW YORK *DAILY ADVERTISER*,
14 MARCH 1789

It is therefore in the peace-administration of Mr. Clinton, that we may expect to find the best materials for judging of his fitness or unfitness to govern. . . . *I do not recollect a single* measure of public utility since the peace, for which the state is indebted to its Chief Magistrate.

H. G. LETTERS NO. 13, NEW YORK DAILY ADVERTISER, 8 APRIL 1789

Viewing in the light I do the conduct of the governor, I consider it as a sacred duty which I owe to the country, to advise all those with whom I have any connection or intercourse to promote a change. It is possible that the governor finding the execution of his schemes impracticable, may have abandoned them. But I conceive a man capable of adopting such views as too dangerous to be trusted at the head of the state.

TO RUFUS KING, PHILADELPHIA, 28 JUNE 1792

I have not, as you will imagine, been inattentive to your political squabble.* I believe you are right (though I have not accurately examined) but I am not without apprehension that a ferment may be raised which may not be allayed when you wish it. Tis not to be forgotten that the opposers of Clinton are the real friends to order & good Government; and that it will ill become them to give an example of the contrary.

*A reference to the disputed New York gubernatorial election in which the incumbent George Clinton defeated his challenger, John Jay, only after the ballots of four counties were disqualified because of irregularities.

TO JOHN ADAMS, PHILADELPHIA, 16 AUGUST 1792

[In speaking about Clinton's parsimoniousness.] You forgot that Mr. Clinton could feast upon what would starve another.

FROM HAMILTON, PHILADELPHIA, 21 SEPTEMBER 1792

Mr. Clinton's success [in winning the vice presidency] I should think very unfortunate. I am not for trusting the Government too much in the hands of its enemies. But still Mr. C—— is a man of property, and, in private life, as far as I know of probity.

TO JOHN STEELE, PHILADELPHIA, 15 OCTOBER 1792
As to Mr. Clinton he is a man of narrow and perverse politics, and as well under the former as under the present Government, he has been steadily since the termination of the war with Great Britain opposed to national principles.

JAMES CLINTON

TO ISRAEL PUTNAM, CORYELL'S FERRY, N.J., 30 JULY 1777
As some person must be found to succeed [George Clinton in command of the forts at the Highlands of the Hudson], He desires me to mention to you General James Clinton, who is, in his present situation, in a manner lost to the service. This Gentleman having been formerly stationed at those posts, is to be supposed well acquainted with them; and he has the character of being a brave man, but it is to be apprehended he may want activity which will be a very essential quality.

JOHN COLLINS

TO JEREMIAH OLNEY, NEW YORK, 6 OCTOBER 1788
. . . as to Your Present Governor, the opinion I have hitherto entertained of his honesty will not permit me to suppose he will not afford his influence with the party to bring about the desirable event [i.e., the calling of a state ratifying convention].

THOMAS CONWAY

TO GEORGE CLINTON, VALLEY FORGE, PA., 13 FEBRUARY 1778
He is one of the vermin bred in the entrails of this chimera dire, and there does not exist a more villainous calumniator and incendiary.

TENCH COXE

TO TIMOTHY PICKERING, NEW YORK, 13 MAY 1790
I can with truth assure you, that you were one of a very small number who held a competition in my judgment and that had personal considerations alone influenced me, I could with difficulty have preferred another. Reasons of a peculiar nature, however, have determined my choice towards Mr. Tench Coxe, who to great industry and very good talents adds an extensive theoretical and practical knowledge of Trade.

TO PRESIDENT GEORGE WASHINGTON, PHILADELPHIA, 2 FEBRUARY 1795
His [Coxe's] statement respecting the Report of a Committee, the discussions in the two houses of Congress & in regard to the provisions of the Act making alterations in the Treasury and War Departments weighs little in my mind. My memory does not serve me to establish or reject the particulars he suggests. I remember however that some points in the report of the Committee, which Mr. Coxe did not like, were introduced without my concurrence, and that I told him so at the time; that his intrigues which have been incessant, in an incessant struggle for preeminence over Mr. Wolcott, had marshalled some personal friends of his with the usual opposers of the department to embarrass the progress of the Bill and give it a complexion favorable to his ambition—that there was a diversity of opinions & that finally the Bill was shaped in conformity with suggestions from me to Individuals.

But I have always viewed Mr. Coxe's pretensions to make the opinions of his friends the standard for the execution of the law as neither modest nor correct.

In fine, I should have thought what Mr. Coxe would have deemed most consistent with the principles of the Department very wrong. I considered him as having already more business confided to him than his talents for execution were equal to a large part of which has since been withdrawn from him at his own pressing request. I considered him as an inferior officer in the department to Mr. Wolcott and after the disposition he had shown I should have regarded it as treating Mr. Wolcott ill to have invested him even with a temporary superiority. In the last place I had much greater confidence in the proper and efficient execution of the business of Mr. Wolcott than by him.

TO OLIVER WOLCOTT, JR., NEW YORK, 5 AUGUST 1795
I do not wonder at what you tell me of the author of a certain piece. That man is too cunning to be wise. I have been so much in the habit of seeing him mistaken that I hold his opinion cheap.

HENRY W. DE SAUSSURE

TO PRESIDENT GEORGE WASHINGTON, NEW YORK,
5 NOVEMBER 1795
Desaussure, I believe, has considerable talents, is of gentlemanlike manners, good views, and only wants sufficient standing to put him upon a footing with any attainable man.

SAMUEL DEXTER AND CHRISTOPHER GORE

TO PRESIDENT GEORGE WASHINGTON, NEW YORK,
5 NOVEMBER 1795
An Attorney General I believe may easily be fixed upon by a satisfactory choice. Either Mr. *Dexter* or Mr. *Gore* would answer. They are both men of undoubted probity. Mr. Dexter has most *natural* talent & is strong in his particular profession.

Mr. Gore is I believe equally considered in his profession & has more various information. No good man doubts Mr. Gore's purity but he has made money by agencies for British Houses in the recovery of debts, etc. and by operations in the funds which a certain party object to him. I believe Mr. Dexter is free from every thing of this kind. Mr. [Rufus] King thinks *Gore* on the whole preferable. I hesitate between them. Either will I think be a good appointment.

WILLIAM DUER

TO WALTER LIVINGSTON, 1796
Poor Duer has now had a long & severe confinement*—Such as would be adequate for no trifling crime. I am well aware of all the blame to which he is liable and do not mean to be his apologist—though I believe he has been as much the dupe of his own imagination as others have been the victims of his projects. But what then? He is a man—he is a man, who with a great deal of good zeal has in critical times rendered valuable services to the Country. He is a husband, who has a most worthy & amiable wife perishing with chagrin at his situation—Your relation by blood—mine by marriage. He is a father who has a number of fine children destitute of the means of education & support every way in need of his future exertions.

These are titles to sympathy, which I shall be mistaken if you do not feel. You are his creditor. Your example may influence others. He wants permission, through a letter of license to breathe the air for *five* years. Your signature to the enclosed draft of One will give me much pleasure.

*Duer had been confined to debtors' prison after his scandalous investment scheme that triggered the Panic of 1793 that caused the financial ruin of many.

HORATIO GATES

TO JOHN LAURENS, MIDDLEBROOK, N.J., APRIL 1779
Gates has refused the Indian command. [John] Sullivan is to take it. The former has lately given a fresh proof of his impudence, his folly and his rascality.

TO JAMES DUANE, BERGEN COUNTY, N.J.,
6 SEPTEMBER 1780
The letter accompanying this has lain by two or three days for want of an opportunity. I have heard since of Gates defeat, a very good comment on the necessity of changing our system. His passion for Militia, I fancy will be a little cured, and he will cease to think them the best bulwark of American liberty. What think you of the conduct of this great man? I am his enemy personally, for unjust and unprovoked attacks upon my character, therefore what I say of him ought to be received as from an enemy, and have no more weight than as it is consistent with fact and common sense. But did ever any one hear of such a disposition or such a flight? His best troops placed on the side strongest by nature, his worst on that weakest by nature, and his attack made with these. 'Tis impossible to give a more complete picture of military absurdity. It is equally against the maxims of war, and common sense. We see the consequence. His left ran away and left his right uncovered. His right wing turned on the left in all probability been cut off. Though in truth the General seems to have known very little what became of his army.

Had he placed his Militia on his right supported by the Morass, and his Continental troops on his left, where it seems he was most vulnerable, his right would have been more secure, and his left would have opposed the enemy; and instead of going backward when he ordered to attack would have gone forward. The reverse of what has happened might have happened.

But was there ever an instance of a General running away as Gates has done from his whole army? and was there ever so precipitous a flight? One hundred and eighty miles in three days and a half. It does admirable credit to the activity of a man at his time of life. But it disgraces the General and the Soldiers. I always believed him to be very far short of a Hector, or an Ulysses. All the world I think will begin to agree with me.

TO ELIZABETH SCHUYLER, BERGEN COUNTY, N.J.,
6 SEPTEMBER 1780

Most people here are groaning under a very disagreeable piece of intelligence just come from the Southward; that Gates has had a total defeat near Camden in South Carolina. Cornwallis and he met in the night of the 15th by accident marching to the same point. The advanced guards skirmished and the two armies halted and formed 'till morning. In the morning a battle ensued, in which the Militia and Gates with them immediately run away and left the Continental troops to contend with the enemy's whole force. They did it obstinately; and probably are most of them cut off. Gates however who writes to Congress seems to know very little what has become of his army. He showed that age and the long labors and fatigues of a military life had not in the least impaired his activity; for in three days and a half, he reached Hillsborough, one hundred and eighty miles from the scene of action, leaving all his troops to take care of themselves, and get out of the scraps as well as they could. He has confirmed in this instance the opinion I always had of him.

WILLIAM BRANCH GILES

TO EDWARD CARRINGTON, PHILADELPHIA, 26 MAY 1792
For a considerable part of the last session [of Congress], Mr. Madison lay in a great measure *perdu* [i.e., absent or missing]. But it was evident from his votes & a variety of little movements and appearances, that he was the prompter of Mr. Giles & others, who were the open instruments of opposition.

WILLIAM GORDON

TO JOHN LAURENS, WEST POINT, N.Y., 11 SEPTEMBER 1779
Speaking of a Caesar & a Cromwell—Don't you think *the Cabal* have reported that I declared in a public house in Philadelphia "it was high time for the people to rise, join General Washington & turn Congress out of Doors." I am running the rogues pretty hard—[Francis] Dana was the first mentioned to me. He has given up Doctor Gordon of Jamaica Plains. You will remember the old Jesuit; he made us a visit at Fredericksburg and is writing the history of America. The proverb is verified—"there never was any mischief but had a *priest* or a woman at the bottom." I doubt not subordination and every species of villainy will be made use of to cover the villainy of the attack. I have written to Gordon and what do you think is his answer?—he will give up his author, if I will pledge my honor "neither to give nor accept a challenge to cause it to be given nor accepted, nor to engage in any recounter that may produce a duel." Pleasant terms enough—I am first to be calumniated and then if my calumniator takes it into his head I am to bear a cudgeling from him with christian patience and forbearance; for the terms required if pursued to their consequences comes to this. I have ridiculed the proposal and insisted on the author, on the principle of *unconditional submission*. What the Doctor's impudence will answer I know not.

TO WILLIAM GORDON, MORRISTOWN, N.J.,
10 DECEMBER 1779

The unravelment of the plot in the ridiculous farce you have been acting proves, as I at first suspected, that you are yourself the author of the calumny; such I consider you and such I shall represent you. The representation I am sure will find credit with all who know me, and the notorious bias of your disposition to duplicity and slander will give it sanction with all who are acquainted with you. I shall use the less ceremony as I am well informed you have established a character which in the opinion of every man of sense has forfeited all title to the delicacy of treatment usually attached to your function [i.e., a minister]. I only lament that respect to myself obliges me to confine the expression of my contempt to words.

CHRISTOPHER GORE

See Samuel Dexter.

NATHANAEL GREENE

EULOGY ON NATHANAEL GREENE, NEW YORK, 4 JULY 1789
He was an accomplished master in the science of military command! . . . The perseverance courage enterprise and resource displayed by the American General . . . commanded the admiration even of his enemies.

ELIZABETH SCHUYLER HAMILTON

TO MARGARITA SCHUYLER, MORRISTOWN, N.J.,
FEBRUARY 1780

She is most unmercifully handsome and so perverse that she has none of those pretty affectations which are the prerogatives of beauty. Her good sense is destitute of that happy mixture of vanity and ostentation which would make it conspicuous to the whole tribe of fools and foplings as well as to men of understanding. . . . In short she is so strange a creature that she possesses all the beauties, virtues, and graces of her sex without any of those amiable defects which from their general prevalence are esteemed by connoisseurs necessary shades in the character of a fine woman.

TO JOHN LAURENS, RAMAPO, N.J., 30 JUNE 1780
Next fall completes my doom. I give up my liberty to Miss Schuyler. She is a good hearted girl who I am sure will never play the termagant; though not a genius she has fine black eyes; is rather handsome and has every other requisite of the exterior to make a lover happy. And believe me, I am lover in earnest, though I do not speak of the perfections of my Mistress in the enthusiasm of chivalry.

TO ELIZABETH SCHUYLER HAMILTON, PREAKNESS, N.J., 2–4 JULY 1780
I love you more and more every hour. The sweet softness and delicacy of your mind and manners, the elevation of your sentiments, the real goodness of your heart, its tenderness to me, the beauties of your face and person, your unpretending good sense, and that innocent simplicity and frankness which pervade your actions—all these appear to me with increasing amiableness and place you in my estimation above all the rest of your sex.

JOHN HANCOCK

TO THEODORE SEDGWICK, NEW YORK, 9 OCTOBER 1788
On the subject of Vice President, my ideas have concurred with your, and I believe Mr. Adams will have the votes of this state. He will certainly, I think, be preferred to the other Gentleman [John Hancock]. Yet, *certainly,* is perhaps too strong a

word. I can conceive that the other, who is supposed to be a more pliable man may command Antifoederal influence.

JAMES INNES

TO PRESIDENT GEORGE WASHINGTON, NEW YORK,
5 NOVEMBER 1795
Mr. Innis, I fear is too absolutely lazy for Secretary of State. The objection would weigh less as to Attorney General.

JONATHAN JACKSON

TO GEORGE THATCHER, PHILADELPHIA, 18 MAY 1793
Mr. Jonathan Jackson—as a man of sense, probity & delicacy & whose impartiality will be drawn into question by no local circumstances.

JOHN JAY

TO JOHN JAY, PHILADELPHIA, 25 JULY 1783
Though I have not performed my promise of writing to you, which I made you when you left this country [in 1779], yet I have not the less interested myself in your welfare and success. I have been witness with pleasure to every event which has had a tendency to advance you in the esteem of your country; and I may assure you with sincerity, that it is as high as you could possibly wish. All have united in the warmest approbation of your conduct. I cannot forbear telling you this, because my situation has given me access to the truth, and I gratify my friendship for you in communicating what cannot fail to gratify your sensibility.

The peace which exceeds in the goodness of its terms, the expectations of the most sanguine does the highest honor to those who made it. It is the more agreeable, as the time was come, when thinking men began to be seriously alarmed at the internal embarrassments and exhausted state of this country. The New England people talk of making you an annual *fish-offering* as an acknowledgement of your exertion for the participation of the fisheries.

TO PRESIDENT GEORGE WASHINGTON, PHILADELPHIA, 14 APRIL 1794

[On the choice of treaty negotiator to Great Britain] I beg leave to add that of the persons whom you would deem free from any constitutional objections—Mr. Jay is the only man in whose qualifications for success there would be thorough confidence and him whom alone it would be advisable to send. I think the business would have the best chance possible in his hands. And I flatter myself that his mission would issue in a manner that would produce the most important good to the Nation.

THOMAS JEFFERSON

TO EDWARD CARRINGTON, PHILADELPHIA, 26 MAY 1792

In France . . . he drank deeply of the French philosophy in religion, in science, in politics. . . . He came electrified *plus* with attachment to France and with the project of knitting together the two countries in the closest political bands. . . .

If I were disposed to promote Monarchy & overthrow State Governments, I would mount the hobby horse of popularity—I would cry out usurpation—danger to liberty &c. &c.—I would endeavor to prostrate the National Government—raise a ferment—and then "ride in the Whirlwind and direct the Storm." That there are men acting with Jefferson & Madison who have this in view I verily believe. I could lay my finger on some of them. That Madison does *not* mean it I also verily believe, and I rather believe the same of Jefferson; but I read him upon the whole thus—"A man of profound ambition & violent passions."

AN AMERICAN NO. I, GAZETTE OF THE UNITED STATES, 4 AUGUST 1792

Mr. Jefferson is emulous of being the head of a party whose politics have constantly aimed at elevating state power upon the ruins of national authority.

"CATULLUS" NO. III, GAZETTE OF THE UNITED STATES, 29 SEPTEMBER 1792

Mr. Jefferson has hitherto been distinguished as the quiet modest, retiring philosopher—as the plain simple unambitious republican. He shall not now for the first time be regarded as the intriguing incendiary—the aspiring turbulent competitor.

How long it is since that gentleman's real character may have *divined,* or whether this is only the *first time* that the *secret* has been disclosed, I am not sufficiently acquainted with the history of his political life to determine; But there is always "a *first time,*" when characters studious of artful disguises are unveiled; When the visor of stoicism is plucked from the brow of the Epicurean; when the plain garb of Quaker simplicity is stripped from the concealed voluptuary; when Caesar *coyly refusing* the proffered diadem, is seen to be Caesar *rejecting* the trappings, but tenaciously grasping the substance of imperial domination.

TO CHARLES COTESWORTH PINCKNEY, PHILADELPHIA, 10 OCTOBER 1792

[It would be unfortunate if Jefferson would defeat Adams as Vice President.] That Gentleman [Jefferson] whom I once very much esteemed, but who does not permit me to retain that sentiment for him, is certainly a man of sublimated and paradoxical imagination—entertaining & propagating notions inconsistent with dignified and orderly Government.

TO JOHN STEELE, PHILADELPHIA, 15 OCTOBER 1792
There was a time when I should have balanced between Mr. Jefferson & Mr. Adams; but I now view the former as a man of sublimated & paradoxical imagination—cherishing notions incompatible with regular and firm government.

TO JEREMIAH WADSWORTH, NEW YORK, 6 NOVEMBER 1796
I perceive you are an elector. In this state we support unanimously John Adams and Thomas Pinckney; on the principle of taking a double chance against *Jefferson,* deeming it far more important that *he* shall *not* be the President than who of the two men, *Adams and Pinckney, shall be* the President. The Government and the national interests will be perfectly safe in the hands of either of these characters. In those of Jefferson there is every thing to fear. Surely then our policy is the true one. 'Tis not a *man* but a *cause* we are to support.

TO RUFUS KING, NEW YORK, 15 FEBRUARY 1797
Mr. Adams is President, Mr. Jefferson Vice President. Our Jacobins say they are well pleased and that the *Lion* & the *Lamb* are to lie down together. Mr. Adams's *personal* friends talk a little in the same way. Mr. *Jefferson* is not half so ill a man as we have been accustomed to think him. There is to be a united and a vigorous administration. Skeptics like me quietly look forward to the event—willing to hope but not prepared to believe. If Mr. Adams has *Vanity* to plan a plot has been laid to take hold of it. We trust his real good sense and integrity will be a sufficient shield.

TO GOVERNOR JOHN JAY, NEW YORK, 7 MAY 1800
[Asking Governor Jay to call a special session of the [New York] legislature to change the [state's] allocation of presidential electors from winner-take-all to district allocation in

order to defeat Jefferson as president in the 1800 election.] In observing this, I shall not be supposed to mean that any thing ought to be done which integrity will forbid—but merely that the scruples of delicacy and propriety, as relative to a common course of things, ought to yield to the extraordinary nature of the crisis. They ought not to hinder the taking of a *legal* and *constitutional* step, to prevent an *Atheist in Religion* and a *Fanatic* in politics from getting possession of the helm of the State.

HAMBDEN, KINGSTON, N.Y., 30 AUGUST 1800
[Referring to essays emanating from Thomas Jefferson] Such a collection of blotched reputations need but be exposed to excite horror. If the tree known by its fruit, why not the fruit by the tree? If the fountain is corrupt, how can pure water be expected to flow from it? Has rottenness entered into the heart, how can the blood remain untainted?

TO JAMES A. BAYARD, NEW YORK, 16 JANUARY 1801
[In comparing Jefferson favorably against Aaron Burr.] Perhaps myself the first, at some expense of popularity, to unfold the true character of Jefferson, it is too late for me to become his apologist. Nor can I have any disposition to do it. I admit that his politics are tinctured with fanaticism, that he is too much in earnest in his democracy, that he has been a mischievous enemy to the principle measures of our past administration, that he is crafty & persevering in his objects, that he is not scrupulous about the means of success, nor very mindful of truth, and that he is a contemptible hypocrite. But it is not true as is alleged that he is an enemy to the power of the Executive, or that he is for confounding all the powers in the House of Representatives. It is a fact which I have frequently mentioned that while we were in the administration together

he was generally for a large construction of the Executive authority, & not backward to act upon it in cases which coincided with his views. Let it be added, that in his theoretic Ideas he has considered as improper the participation of the Senate in the Executive Authority. I have more than once made the reflection that viewing himself as the reversioner, he was solicitous to come into possession of a Good Estate. Nor is it true that Jefferson is zealot enough to do anything in pursuance of his principles which will contravene his popularity, or his interest. He is as likely as any man I know to temporize—to calculate what will be likely to promote his own reputation and advantage; and the probable result of such a temper is the preservation of systems, though originally opposed, which being once established, could not be overturned without danger to the person who did it. To my mind a true estimate of Mr. J's. character warrants the expectation of a temporizing rather than a violent system. That Jefferson has manifested a culpable predilection for France is certainly true; but I think it a question whether it did not proceed quite as much from her *popularity* among us, as from sentiment, and in proportion as that popularity is diminished his zeal will cool. Add to this that there is no fair reason to suppose him capable of being corrupted, which is a security that he will not go beyond certain limits. It is not at all improbable that under the change of circumstances Jefferson's Gallicism has considerably abated.

SAMUEL JONES

TO HUGH SETON, NEW YORK, 18 JUNE 1784
[On obtaining a lawyer to represent a friend of Seton's.] I thought it my duty to transfer the trust to some person on the spot to whose judgment and integrity your interests might be safely committed. I have fixed upon Mr. Samuel Jones for this

purpose; a Gentleman as distinguished for his probity as for his professional knowledge.

TO TIMOTHY PICKERING, NEW YORK, 17 MARCH 1798
If Robert Troupe resigns his office of District Judge The President cannot make a better choice than of Samuel Jones Esqr. the present comptroller of the State. I understand he will accept.

RUFUS KING

TO JOHN JAY, PHILADELPHIA, 3 SEPTEMBER 1792
Perhaps it will not be amiss for you to converse with Mr. King. His judgment is sound; he has caution and energy.

TO TIMOTHY PICKERING, NEW YORK, 10 MAY 1796
[In suggesting Rufus King as a replacement for Thomas Pinckney as U.S. minister to Great Britain.] While I have my pen in my hand, give me leave to mention a particular subject to you. Mr. Pinckney, it is said, desires to return to the U. States. In this case a successor will be wanted. If we had power to make a man for the purpose, we could not imagine a fitter than Mr. *King*. He is tired of the Senate & I fear will resign at all events. I presume he would accept the mission to England. Can there be a doubt that it will be wise to offer it to him?

TO PRESIDENT GEORGE WASHINGTON, NEW YORK, 10 MAY 1796
It is rumored, that Mr. Pinckney entertains a wish to return to this Country. Give me leave to make known to you, that in such an event, I have ground to believe it would not be disagreeable to Mr. *King* to be the successor. I verily believe, that a more fit man for the purpose cannot be found and I imagine

Mr. King will in every event leave the Senate. Should you think well of his appointment, I presume he would be disposed by a *previous resignation* to make the way easy to his nomination by you. Considering the strong commercial relations of the two countries it is truly very important that each should have with the other a man able and willing to give fair play to reciprocal interests.

TO PRESIDENT GEORGE WASHINGTON, NEW YORK,
20 MAY 1796

I observe what you say on the subject of a certain diplomatic mission. Permit me to offer with frankness the reflections which have struck my mind.

The importance to our security and commerce of good understanding with G. Britain renders it very important that a man *able* and *not disagreeable* to that Government should be there. The Gentleman in question equally with any who could go & better than any willing to go answers this description. The idea hinted in your letter will apply to every man fit for the mission by his conspicuousness, talents and dispositions. 'Tis the stalking horse of a certain party & is made use of against every man who is not in their view & of sufficient consequence to attract their obloquy. If listened to, it will deprive the Government of the services of the most able and faithful agents. Is this expedient? What will be gained by it? Is it not evident that this party will pursue its hostility at all events as far as public opinion will permit? Does policy require any thing more than that they shall have no real cause to complain? Will it do, in deference to their calumniating insinuations to forbear employing the most competent men or to entrust the great business of the Country to unskillful unfaithful or doubtful hands? I really feel a conviction that it will be very dangerous to let party insinuations of this kind prove a serious obstacle to the employment of the best qualified characters.

Mr. King is a remarkably well informed man—a very judicious one—a man of address—a man of fortune and economy whose situation affords just ground of confidence—a man of unimpeached probity where he is best known—a firm friend to the Government—a supporter of the measures of the President—a man who cannot but feel that he has strong pretensions to confidence and trust.

TO ANGELICA SCHUYLER CHURCH, NEW YORK,
25 JUNE 1796
I wrote you last by Mr. King who sailed a few days since for London as our Minister Plenipotentiary. You must not think the less well of him for not being a Jacobin—for he is a very clever fellow and will do credit to your Country.

HENRY KNOX

TO GEORGE WASHINGTON, PHILADELPHIA,
13 FEBRUARY 1783
General Knox has the confidence of the army & is a man of sense. I think he may be safely made use of. Situated as I am Your Excellency will feel the confidential nature of these observations.

TO JAMES MADISON, NEW YORK, 23 NOVEMBER 1788
As to Knox [for U.S. Vice President] I cannot persuade myself that he will incline to the appointment. He must *sacrifice* emolument by it which must *of necessity* be a primary object with him.

TO EDWARD CARRINGTON, PHILADELPHIA, 26 MAY 1792
Poor *Knox* has come in for a share of their [Madison and Jefferson's] persecution as a man who generally thinks with me & who has a portion of the President's good Will & confidence.

HENRY KUHL

TO THOMAS WILLING, ALBANY, N.Y., 5 APRIL 1795
Mr. Henry Kuhl, Principal Clerk in the Comptroller's office has informed me that he is a candidate for the place of Assistant Cashier to the Bank of the United States and has requested a testimonial of my opinion of his qualifications.

I without scruple give it and in the strongest manner; I cannot imagine a man better qualified for such a place than he is. A thorough knowledge of accounts—a very clear *business head*—remarkable steadiness, attention, diligence and *accuracy* mark him out as a man peculiarly fitted for such an employment. And my opinion of his integrity and trust-worthiness is equal to that of his capacity. Indeed I do not scruple to say that I am persuaded he will be found a valuable acquisition to the institution. It is not often that such a man will present himself.

MARQUIS DE LAFAYETTE

TO JAMES DUANE, MORRISTOWN, N.J., 14 MAY 1780
The Marquis has a title to all the love of all America; but you know he has a thousand little whims to satisfy—one of these he *will have* me to write to some friend in Congress about. He is desirous of having the Captain of the Frigate in which he came complimented and gives several pretty instances of his punctuality & disinterestedness. He wishes Congress to pass some resolutions of thanks & to recommend him to their Minister in France, to be recommended to the French Court. The first of these is practicable. The last I think might have an officious appearance. The *essential* services the Marquis has rendered America in France give him a claim for all that can be done with propriety; but Congress must not commit themselves.

TO THE MARQUIS DE LAFAYETTE, NEW YORK,
6 JANUARY 1799
I have been made happy my dear friend by the receipt of your letter of the 12th of August last. No explanation of your political principles was necessary to satisfy me of the perfect consistency and purity of your conduct. The interpretation may always be left to my attachment for you. Whatever difference of opinion may on any occasion exist between us can never lessen my conviction of the goodness both of your head and heart. . . . Neither have I abandoned the idea that 'tis most advisable for you to remain in Europe 'till the difference is adjusted [between France and America]. It would be very difficult for you here to steer a course which would not place you in a party and remove you from the broad ground which you now occupy in the hearts of all. It is a favorite point with me that you shall find in the universal regard of this country all the consolations which the loss of your own (for so I consider it) may render requisite.

JOHN LANSING, JR.

TO ROBERT MORRIS, ALBANY, N.Y., 13 AUGUST 1782
Lansing is a good young fellow and a good practitioner of the law, but his friends mistook his talents when they made him a statesman. He thinks two pence an ounce upon plate a *monstrous tax*. The county of Albany is not of my opinion concerning him.

TO ROBERT G. HARPER, ALBANY, N.Y., 19 FEBRUARY 1804
One consequence of the distraction of the party is the declining of Governor Clinton to be candidate [for governor] at the next election. A very respectable man as to private character, Chancellor Lansing, is the substitute. He had secretly many competitors and is far from being a general favorite of the party.

From this moment, it is destined to be split into fragments, unless hereafter reunited under the more skillful and able lead of Mr. Burr.

JOHN LAURANCE

TO ROBERT MORRIS, ALBANY, N.Y., 13 AUGUST 1782
Laurance is a man of good sense and good intentions—has just views of public affairs—is active and accurate in business. He is from conviction an advocate for strengthening the Federal government and for reforming the vices of our interior administration.

HENRY "LIGHTHORSE HARRY" LEE

TO PRESIDENT GEORGE WASHINGTON, NEW YORK, 5 NOVEMBER 1795
Governor Lee has several things for him & several against him—he ought to have a good secretary under him.

TO TIMOTHY PICKERING, NEW YORK, 20 NOVEMBER 1795
Of those South, notwithstanding there are real and weighty objections, I incline on the whole to LEE.

DAVID LENOX AND FRANCIS NICHOLS

TO PRESIDENT GEORGE WASHINGTON, PHILADELPHIA, 14 JUNE 1794
Colo. Nichols & Major Lenox stand nearly on a level—both men of adequate understanding, honorable characters, some property, undoubted firmness, & probable exertion, but on the last point there is greater assurance of Major Lenox. But neither of these gentlemen seem to have that extensive notoriety & popularity of character which is desirable to assist the pro-

gress of disagreeable laws. In this particular Mr. [Henry] Miller or Mr. [Charles] Biddle has greatly the advantage.

JAMES McHENRY

TO JAMES DUANE, PREAKNESS, NJ, 22 JULY 1780
I take the liberty my Dear Sir to request your interest for a friend of mine and a member of the [Washington military] family, Dr. McHenry. He wishes to quit a Station which among foreigners is not viewed in a very reputable light and to get into one more military. He will go into the Marquis's family as an aide. He has been in the army since the commencement of the War—first in the medical line, since the 15th of May 78, as a *Secretary* to the Commander in Chief. You know him to be a man of Sense and merit. A more intimate acquaintance with him makes me hold him as such in an eminent degree. He has now no military existence properly speaking—no rank. I believe he is not immoderate. For my own part were I to decide for him considering his length of services, his merit, the relation in which he has stood, I would give him a Majority [i.e., a rank of major]. I have no doubt my Dear Sir, you will be glad to serve Mr. McHenry from motives of justice, of friendship to him and (shall I not add) of friendship to me.

TO PRESIDENT GEORGE WASHINGTON, NEW YORK,
5 NOVEMBER 1795
McHenry you know he would give no strength to the administration but he would not disgrace the Office [of Secretary of War]—his views are good—perhaps his health &c. would prevent his accepting.

TO OLIVER WOLCOTT, JR., NEW YORK, 15 JUNE 1796
After turning the thing over and Over in my mind I know of nothing better that you have in your power than to send Mc-

Henry [on a diplomatic mission to France]. He is not yet obnoxious to the French and has been understood formerly to have had some kindness towards their Revolution. His present Office [Secretary of War] would give a sort of importance to the mission. If he should incline to an absolute relinquishment his mission might be temporary & Col. Pickering could carry on his Office in his absence. He is at hand & might depart immediately & I believe he would explain very well & do no foolish thing.

TO PRESIDENT GEORGE WASHINGTON, PHILADELPHIA,
29 JULY 1798

But, My Dear Sir. There is a matter of far greater moment than all this which I must do violence to my friendship by stating to you; but of which it is essential you should be apprised. It is that my friend, McHenry, is wholly insufficient for his place [as Secretary of War], with the additional misfortune of not having himself the least suspicion of the fact! This generally will not surprise you, when you take into view the large scale upon which he is now to act. But you perhaps may not be aware of the whole extent of the insufficiency. It is so great as to leave no probability that the business of the War Department can make any tolerable progress in his hands. This has been long observed; and has been more than once mentioned to the President [John Adams] by members of Congress. He is not insensible, I believe, that the execution of the department does not produce the expected results; but the case is of course delicate and embarrassing.

My real friendship for McHenry concurring with my zeal for the service predisposed me to aid him in all that he could properly throw upon me. And I thought that he would have been glad in the organization of the army and in the conduct of the recruiting service, to make me useful to him. With this view I came to this City & I previously opened the way, as far as I could with the least decency. But the idea has been thus far very partially embraced and tomorrow or the next day I shall return to New York without much fruit of my journey. I mention this purely to apprise you of the course of things and the probable results. It is to be regretted that the supposition of cooperation between the Secretary at War and the principal military officers will unavoidably throw upon the latter a part of the blame which the ill success of the operations of the war department may be expected to produce. Thus you perceive, Sir, your perplexities are begun.

JAMES MADISON

TO EDWARD CARRINGTON, PHILADELPHIA, 26 MAY 1792
Mr. Madison cooperating with Mr. Jefferson . . . have a womanish attachment to France and a womanish resentment against Great Britain. . . .

Mr. Madison cooperating with Mr. Jefferson is at the head of a faction decidedly hostile to me and my administration and actuated by views in my judgment subversive of the principles of good government and dangerous to the union, peace, and happiness of the Country. . . .

The opinion I once entertained of the candour and simplicity and fairness of Mr. Madison's character has, I acknowledge, given way to a decided opinion that *it is one of a peculiarly artificial and complicated kind.* . . .

Mr. Madison's true character is the reverse of that *simple, fair, candid one,* which he has assumed.

WILLIAM MALCOLM

TO ISRAEL PUTNAM, CORYELL'S FERRY, N.J., 30 JULY 1777
Colonel Malcolm is an active, judicious man, and seems to have some skill in fortifications, and a turn for those things

which it will be necessary to attend to at the posts to be commanded by General [James] Clinton.

TO PRESIDENT OF CONGRESS JOHN JAY,
NEW WINDSOR, N.Y., 26 JUNE 1779
We have compared our ideas of Col. Malcolm's character and they are not very dissimilar. I shall only observe that he is a man of talents, of a military turn, of attention, activity and method in business. He is now out of the service, I believe from misconception. He thought himself neglected by Congress, by his not having been appointed in the first instance to the command of the incorporated regiments. I won't say that there was not a little caprice and impatience on his side. The history of a man's importance to himself is pretty strongly marked in most parts of his conduct. I have reason to think he repents his having thrown himself out of the service, and is uneasy in his present negative situation. He has signified to me a wish either to be reintroduced or placed in the Board of war. The first is in my opinion impossible without giving much discontent; the last is I think desirable. I am persuaded he would be *very useful* as a member of that board—as much so as any man I am acquainted with. Besides his utility in this capacity, if I am not mistaken, it will be good policy to employ him somewhere out of the State [of New York]. He is of a restless temper, artful, plausible and popular, addicted to cabal. As he did not make your government, it is not entirely to his palate and some few changes would give better security to the liberties of the people.

TO PRESIDENT OF CONGRESS JOHN JAY, WEST POINT, N.Y.,
29 SEPTEMBER 1779
I feel the force of your scruples respecting a certain Gentleman; and while you entertain the doubts you intimate, it certainly

would not be reconcilable to a regard for the public good to promote his appointment. My recommendation, besides motives of particular policy, was founded upon an opinion that he would really be useful in the station. Though I think his character defective and unamiable in many respects I have no suspicion of his fidelity and attachment to the *common* cause—indeed I am persuaded these may be relied upon; and as I had a high idea of his ability, industry and proficiency in the knowledge of men and business, I was induced on principle as well as policy to wish to see him a member of the board. The only subject of hesitation in my mind was his vanity, and consequently an extreme partiality to his own opinions, an impatience of control and a fondness for dominion. I should be apprehensive, if he could not rule the board, he would perplex it, but as he has the art of conciliating those with whom he is connected and is clear sighted in discerning and pursuing his interest, I thought these would overcome the dispositions I have mentioned and teach him the necessity of cultivating harmony with his colleagues.

TO SUPERINTENDENT OF FINANCE ROBERT MORRIS, ALBANY, N.Y., 13 AUGUST 1782

Malcolm has a variety of abilities: he is industrious and expert in business; he wants not resource and is pretty right on the subjects of the day; but he is too fond of popularity and too apt to think every scheme bad, that is not his own. He is closely linked with [John Morin] Scot, because he can govern him: A man of warm passions, he can control all but his vanity, which often stands in the way of his interest. He is accused of duplicity and insincerity. He has it in his power to support or perplex measures, as he may incline, and it will be politic to make it his interest to incline to what is right. It was on this principle I proposed him for a certain office.

THOMAS MARSHALL

TO PETER COLT, PHILADELPHIA, 10 APRIL 1793
Marshall is an essential [to the Society of Establishing Useful Manufactures], and I believe a very deserving man. I think his salary ought to be increased.

HENRY MILLER

TO PRESIDENT GEORGE WASHINGTON, PHILADELPHIA, 14 JUNE 1794
Of the persons named [as possible supervisor for Pennsylvania], Colo. Miller, all circumstances considered, has the judgment of the Secretary in his favor. All agree that he is a man of good character, of friendly dispositions to the Government & Laws of the United States—of industry, exertion, *address & distinguished firmness*—of adequate, though not superior ability, and most likely of any man on whom equal dependence can be placed, to have weight in the most refractory scene of this State. He is also a man of decent property unembarrassed. Among those who *warmly* recommend him is Mr. Ross, Senator of this State, who lives in one of the most western Counties. . . .

Among the persons who have been consulted is the Attorney General [William Bradford]. He gave a preference to Mr. Miller. His knowledge of State characters is diffusive & accurate. Mr. Miller was lately a very promising candidate for the place of *Sentor* in the Senate of the United States.

JAMES MONROE

TO JOHN LAURENS, MIDDLEBROOK, N.J., 22 MAY 1779
Monroe is just setting out from Head Quarters and proposes to go in quest adventures to the Southward. He seems to be

as much of a knight errant as your worship; but as he is an honest fellow, I shall be glad he may find some employment, that will enable him to get knocked in the head in an honorable way. He will relish your black scheme* if any thing handsome can be done for him in that line. You know him to be a man of honor a sensible man and a soldier. This makes it unnecessary to me to say any thing to interest your friendship for him. You love your country too and he has zeal and capacity to serve it.

*Laurens was trying to get approval to raise black battalions.

GOUVERNEUR MORRIS

TO PRESIDENT GEORGE WASHINGTON, NEW YORK, 30 SEPTEMBER 1790

I had lately a visit from a certain Gentleman [British agent George Beckwith] the sole object of which was to make some observations of a delicate nature, which, as they were doubtless intended for your ear, and (such as they are) ought to be known to you, it is of course my duty to communicate.

He began (in a manner somewhat embarrassed which betrayed rather more than he seemed to intend to discover) by telling me that in different companies where he had happened to be, in this City (a circumstance by the way very unlikely) he had heard it mentioned that that other Gentleman [Gouverneur Morris] was upon terms of very great intimacy with the representative of a certain Court [the Marquis de la Luzerne, French minister to Great Britain] at the once where he was employed and with the head of the party opposed to the Minister [Charles James Fox]; and he proceeded to say, that if there were symptoms of backwardness or coolness in the Minister [William Pitt], it had occurred to him that they might possibly be occasioned by such an intimacy; that he had no intimation however of this being the case, and that the idea suggested by him was mere matter of conjecture; that he did not even know it as a fact that the intimacy subsisted. But if this should be the case (said he) you will readily imagine that it cannot be calculated to inspire confidence or facilitate free communication. It would not be surprising, if a very close connection with the representative of another power should beget doubts and reserves; or if a very familiar intercourse with the head of the opposition should occasion prejudice and distance. Man, after all, is but man, and though the Minister has a great mind, and is as little likely as most men to entertain illiberal distrusts or jealousies; yet there is no saying what might be the effect of such conduct upon him. It is hardly possible not to have some diffidence of those, who seem to be very closely united with our political or personal enemies or rivals. At any rate, such an intimacy, if it exists, can do no good, may do some harm. This, as far as I recollect, was the substance of what he said. My answer was nearly as follows.

I have never heard a syllable Sir, about the matter you mention. It appears to me however very possible that an intimacy with both the persons you mention may exist: With the first, because the situation of the parties had naturally produced such an intimacy, while both were in this Country; and to have dropped and avoided it there, would not have been without difficulty, on the score of politeness, and would have worn an extraordinary and mysterious aspect: With the last, from the patronage of American affairs, which is understood to have been uniformly the part of that Gentleman, and in some degree, from a similarity of dispositions and characters; both brilliant men, men of wit and genius; both fond of the pleasures of society. It is to be hoped that appearances, which admit of so easy a solution will not prove an obstacle to any thing which mutual interest dictates—It is impossible that there can be any thing wrong; but that as trifles often mar great affairs he thought it best to impart to me his conjecture, that such use might be made of it as should be thought advisable.

TO RUFUS KING, NEW YORK, 2 OCTOBER 1798
Why does not Gouverneur Morris come home? His talents are wanted. Men like him do not superabound.

RICHARD MORRIS

TO ROBERT MORRIS, ALBANY, N.Y., 13 AUGUST 1782
Mr. Morris the chief Justice is a well meaning man.

ROBERT MORRIS

TO ROBERT MORRIS, DE PEYSTER'S POINT, N.Y., 30 APRIL 1781
I hope Sir you will not consider it as a compliment when I assure you that I heard with the greatest satisfaction of your nomination to the department of finance. In a letter of mine last summer to Mr. [James] Duane, urging among other things the plan of an executive ministry, I mentioned you as the person, who ought to fill that department. I know of no other in America who unites so many advantages, and of course, every impediment to your acceptance is to me a subject of chagrin. I flatter myself Congress will not preclude the public from your services by an obstinate refusal of reasonable conditions; and as one deeply interested in the event I am happy in believing you will not easily be discouraged from undertaking an office, by which you may render America and the world no less a service than the establishment of American independence! Tis by introducing order into our finances—by restoring public credit—not by gaining battles, that we are finally to gain our

object. Tis by putting ourselves in a condition to continue the war not by temporary, violent and unnatural efforts to bring it to a decisive issue, that we shall in reality bring it to a speedy and successful one. In the frankness of truth I believe, Sir, you are the Man best capable of performing this great work.

ALEXANDER HAMILTON: THE CONTINENTALIST NO. IV, *NEW YORK PACKET*, 30 AUGUST 1781

Congress have wisely appointed a superintendent of their finances, a man of acknowledged abilities and integrity, as well as of great personal credit and pecuniary influence.

TO GEORGE WASHINGTON, PHILADELPHIA, 8 APRIL 1783

As to Mr. Morris, I will give Your Excellency a true explanation of his conduct. He had been for some time pressing Congress to endeavor to obtain funds, and had found a great backwardness in the business. He found the taxes unproductive in the different states—he found the loans in Europe making a very slow progress—he found himself pressed on all hands for supplies; he found himself in short reduced to this alternative either of making engagements which he could not fulfill or declaring his resignation in case funds were not established by a given time. Had he followed the first course the bubble must soon have burst—he must have sacrificed his credit & his character, and public credit already in a ruinous condition would have lost its last support. He wisely judged it better to resign; this might increase the embarrassments of the moment, but the necessity of the case it was to be hoped would produce the proper measures; and he might then resume the direction of the machine with advantage and success. He also had some hope that his resignation would prove a stimulus to Congress.

He was however ill-advised in the publication of his letters of resignation. This was an imprudent step and has given a handle to his personal enemies, who by playing upon the passions of others have drawn some well meaning men into the cry against him. But Mr. Morris certainly deserves a great deal from his country. I believe no man in this country but himself could have kept the money-machine a going during the period he has been in office. From every thing that appears his administration has been upright as well as able.

FRANCIS NICHOLS

See David Lenox.

JOSEPH NOURSE

TO PRESIDENT GEORGE WASHINGTON, PHILADELPHIA,
17 APRIL 1791

In contemplating the appointment of the Auditor [Oliver Wolcott, Jr.] as Comptroller, a question naturally arises concerning a substitute for the former. In forming your Judgment on this point you would probably desire to know what may be the pretensions of the next officer in the department below the Auditor namely the Register. I say nothing of the Assistant Secretary or the Treasury, because neither of them I presume would think the place of Auditor an eligible exchange for that which he now has & because I regard them both as distinct & irrelative branches of the department. The Register is a most excellent officer in his place. He has had a great deal of experience in the department, is a perfect accountant & a very upright man. But I cannot say that I am convinced he would make as good an Auditor as he does a Register. I fear he would fail on the score of firmness & I am not sure that his mind is formed for a systematic adherence to principle. I believe at the same time that he is perfectly content to remain where he is.

JEREMIAH OLNEY

TO JEREMIAH OLNEY, PHILADELPHIA, 2 APRIL 1793

You will receive by this opportunity an official Letter. The present you will consider as a private and friendly one.

You will readily believe me, when I assure you, that all my prepossessions are in your favor, and that if there have been any faults on your side, I am ready to ascribe them to the *excesses* of virtues and good qualities, rather than to their *opposites*.

But you will, I am sure, consider it as an act of friendship when I tell you that some good men, who esteem you and think highly of your conduct, in the main, have expressed to me an idea that it has been in some instances too *punctilious,* and not sufficiently accommodating.

I am aware that in a scene where they have been accustomed to much relaxation, a spirit of exactness is particularly necessary, and that *only* a due degree of it may seem rigor. And I have thus construed the intimations alluded to.

But on the other hand I have considered it as possible that your ideas of precise conformity to the laws, may have kept you from venturing upon relaxations in cases in which, from *very special* circumstances, they may have been proper.

My own maxims of conduct are not favorable to much discretion, but cases do sometimes occur in which a little may be indispensable. The exercise of it must always be at the peril of the officer, and therefore ought to stand on manifest ground. But wherever it should appear to have been discreetly and prudently exercised, upon an *urgent* occasion, due allowances would be made for it.

I should be cautious in making such a remark to many officers—because I should fear an abuse—but with you, I have no apprehension, as I am sure your bias is, as it ought to be, towards a strict execution of the laws and your instructions.

The good will of the Merchants is very important in many senses, and if it can be secured without any improper sacrifice or introducing a looseness of practice, it is desirable to do it. Tis impossible for me to define the degree of accommodation which will avoid one extreme or another. This your own judgment, as *special* cases arise, must point out to you. I only mean to convey to you a general sentiment.

EPHRAIM PAINE

TO ROBERT MORRIS, ALBANY, N.Y., 13 AUGUST 1782
[Paine] is a man of strong natural parts and as strong prejudices; his zeal is fiery, his obstinacy unconquerable. He is as primitive in his notions, as in his appearance. Without education, he wants [i.e., needs] more knowledge, or more tractableness.

NATHANIEL PENDLETON

TO PRESIDENT GEORGE WASHINGTON, NEW YORK,
5 NOVEMBER 1795
Judge Pendleton of Georgia . . . writes well, is of respectable abilities and a Gentlemanlike smooth man. If I were sure of his political views I should be much disposed to advise his appointment under the circumstances. But I fear he has been somewhat tainted with the prejudices of Mr. Jefferson & Mr. Madison & I have afflicting suspicions concerning these men.

TO TIMOTHY PICKERING, NEW YORK, 20 NOVEMBER 1795
Since writing the above Judge Pendleton of Georgia has occurred to me [as Secretary of State]. He was a military man—Aide to General Greene & esteemed by him. He is certainly a man of handsome abilities. I have however within a few days

heard that he had some agency in the purchase of the Georgia lands [i.e., Yazoo lands]. If he has had any interested concern in this transaction it would be an immense objection. Otherwise, if he would accept, all things considered I should prefer him [as Secretary of State]. He is tinctured with Jeffersonian Politics but I should be mistaken, if among good men & better informed, he did not go right.

TIMOTHY PICKERING

TO PRESIDENT GEORGE WASHINGTON NEW YORK,
5 NOVEMBER 1796
I am the more particular in these observations because I know that Mr. Pickering, who is a very worthy man, has nevertheless something warm and angular in his temper & will require much a vigilant moderating eye.

CHARLES COTESWORTH PINCKNEY

TO OLIVER WOLCOTT, JR., NEW YORK, 5 APRIL 1797
Pinckney is a man of honor & loves his Country.

THOMAS PINCKNEY

ALEXANDER HAMILTON: *LETTER CONCERNING THE PUBLIC CONDUCT AND CHARACTER OF JOHN ADAMS,* NEW YORK, 24 OCTOBER 1800
It was evidently of much consequence to endeavor to have an eminent Federalist Vice-President. Mr. Thomas Pinckney, of South Carolina, was selected for this purpose. This gentleman, too little known in the North, had been all his lifetime distinguished in the South, for the mildness and amiableness of his manners, the rectitude and purity of his morals, and the sound-

ness and correctness of his understanding, accompanied by a habitual discretion and self-command, which has often occasioned a parallel to be drawn between him and the venerated Washington. In addition to these recommendations, he had been, during a critical period, our Minister at the Court of London, and recently Envoy Extraordinary to the Court of Spain; and in both these trusts, he had acquitted himself to the satisfaction of all parties. With the Court of Spain he had effected a Treaty, which removed all the thorny subjects of contention, that had so long threatened the peace of the two countries, and stipulated for the United States, on their Southern frontier, and on the Mississippi, advantages of real magnitude and importance. . . . My position was, that if chance should decide in favor of Mr. Pinckney, it probably would not be a misfortune; since he, to every essential qualification for the office, added a temper far more discreet and conciliatory than that of Mr. Adams.

ZEPHANIAH PLATT

TO ROBERT MORRIS, ALBANY, N.Y., 13 AUGUST 1782
[Platt] is a man of plain sense, thoroughly acquainted with agriculture. He intends to do well whenever he can hit upon what is right.

ISRAEL PUTNAM

TO GEORGE WASHINGTON, NEW WINDSOR, N.Y.,
10 NOVEMBER 1777
Governor [George] Clinton will do every thing in his power. I wish General Putnam was recalled from the command of this post, and Governor Clinton would accept it. The blunders and caprices of the former are endless.

TO GEORGE WASHINGTON, NEW WINDSOR, N.Y.,
12 NOVEMBER 1777

I believe the past delay is not owing to any fault of his [i.e. General Enoch Poor], but is wholly chargeable on General Putnam. Indeed, Sir, I owe it to the service to say that every part of this Gentleman's conduct is marked with blunders and negligence, and gives general disgust.

EDMUND RANDOLPH

TO PRESIDENT GEORGE WASHINGTON, NEW YORK,
16 OCTOBER 1795

There is another subject upon which I will hazard a few words. It is that of Mr. Randolph. I have seen the intercepted letter, which I presume led to his resignation. I read it with regret, but without much surprise for I never had confidence in Mr. Randolph, and I thought there were very suspicious appearances about him on the occasion to which the letter particularly refers.

DAVID RITTENHOUSE

TO PRESIDENT GEORGE WASHINGTON, TREASURY DEPT.,
PHILADELPHIA, 31 JANUARY 1795

I cannot help thinking that with due exertion the business of the Mint might have been far more matured, and its present powers of Action far greater than they are: And I am led to fear that as long as it continues under its present management the public expectation will be disappointed. The Director, though a most respectable & excellent man, can hardly be expected on several accounts to give that close and undivided attention to it which in its first stages is indispensable.

JOHN RUTLEDGE

TO RUFUS KING, NEW YORK, 14 DECEMBER 1795
[On the Senate's confirmation hearing on Rutledge as the chief justice of the United States.] An extraordinary press of occupation has delayed an answer to your letter on the subject of Mr. R. Though it may come too late, I comply with your request as soon as I can.

The subject is truly a perplexing one; my mind has several times fluctuated. If there was nothing in the case but his imprudent sally upon a certain occasion, I should think the reasons for letting him pass would outweigh those for opposing his passage. But if it be really true—that he is sottish or that his mind is otherwise deranged, or that he has exposed himself by improper conduct in pecuniary transactions, the bias of my judgment would be to negative. And as to the facts I would satisfy myself by careful inquiry of persons of character who may have had an opportunity of knowing.

It is now, and in certain probable events will still more be, of infinite consequence that our Judiciary should be well composed. Reflection upon this in its various aspects weighs heavily in my mind against Mr. R., upon the accounts I have received of him, and balances very weighty consideration the other way.

PHILIP SCHUYLER

TO ROBERT R. LIVINGSTON, HEADQUARTERS NEAR GERMANTOWN, PA., 7 AUGUST 1777
I have been always a very partial Judge of General Schuyler's Conduct, and Vindicated it frequently from the Charges brought against it, but I am at last forced to suppose him Inadequate to the Important Command with which he has been Entrusted. There seems to be a want of firmness in all

his Actions, and this last Instance in my Opinion is too unequivocal to be doubted. The Reason assigned for his last retreat is the panic among the army, which he seems to say is beyond any thing that ever was known, and Mentions an Instance of 300 Men running away from about 50 Indians. . . . Under the best, Leaders may be seized with a sudden panic that may precipitate them into the most cowardly behavior for the Moment, but a settled durable panic is generally a Reflection upon the Leader.

TO ELIZABETH HAMILTON, LIGHT CAMP, N.Y.,
16 AUGUST 1781
I have received my beloved Betsey your letter informing me of the happy escape of your father. He showed an admirable presence of mind, and has given his friends a double pleasure arising from the manner of saving himself and his safety. Upon the whole I am glad this unsuccessful attempt [to kidnap him] has been made. It will prevent his hazarding himself hereafter as he has been accustomed to do. He is a character too valuable to be trifled with, and owes it to his country and to his family to be upon his guard.

TO ELIZABETH HAMILTON, ALBANY, N.Y.,
26 OCTOBER 1796
Your father is really better and as I hope in no present danger. His breathing out looks less & less like mortification & his appetite, strength & spirits are good. A fit of the gout will probably relieve him from the breaking out.

JOHN MORIN SCOTT

TO ROBERT MORRIS, ALBANY, N.Y., 13 AUGUST 1782
Mr. Scot you also know. He has his little objects and his little party. Nature gave him genius; but *habit* has impaired it. He

never had judgment; he now has scarcely plausibility; his influence is just extensive enough to embarrass measures he does not like; and his only aim seems to be by violent professions of popular principles to acquire a popularity which has hitherto coyly eluded his pursuit. His views as a statesman are warped; his principles as a man are said to be not the purest.

WILLIAM LOUGHTON SMITH

TO CHARLES COTESWORTH PINCKNEY, PHILADELPHIA,
10 OCTOBER 1792

Some valuable characters are about to be lost to the House of Representatives of their own choice. I feared once that this would be the case with Mr. Smith of your state; but I believe his present intention is rather to continue to serve. I trust there can be no doubt of his success and I wish means to be used to determine his acquiescence. He is truly an excellent member—a ready clear speaker of a sound analytic head and the justest views—I know no man whose loss from the House would be more severely felt by the good cause.

WILLIAM STEPHENS SMITH

TO PRESIDENT GEORGE WASHINGTON, NEW YORK,
5 NOVEMBER 1795

But for a Secretary of State I know not what to say. *Smith* though not of full size is very respectable for talent & has pretty various information. I think he has more real talent than the last incumbent of the Office [Edmund Randolph]. But there are strong objections to his appointment. I fear he is of an uncomfortable temper. He is popular with no description of men from a certain *hardness* of character and he more than most other men is considered as tinctured with prejudices towards the British. In this particular his ground is somewhat peculiar. It may suit party views to say much of other men but more in this respect is *believed* with regard to Smith. I speak merely as to *bias* and *prejudice*. There are things, & important things for which I would recommend Smith; thinking well of his abilities, information & integrity—but at the present juncture I believe his appointment to the office in question would be unadvisable.

TO OLIVER WOLCOTT, JR., ALBANY, N.Y., 22 APRIL 1797
[Considering a nominee for position of Collector of the Port of New York] I should have mentioned Col. Smith among the most prominent but for the late unfortunate circumstances which attend him and which would render his appointment ineligible to such an Office at this time.

BARON FREDRICH WILHELM VON STEUBEN

TO GEORGE WASHINGTON, NEW YORK, 25 NOVEMBER 1785
The Poor *Baron* is still soliciting Congress, and has every prospect of Indigence before him. He has his imprudencies; but upon the whole he has rendered valuable services; and his merits and the reputation of the Country alike demand that he should not be left to suffer want. If there could be any mode by which Your influence could be employed in his favor; by writing to Your friends in Congress or otherwise, The Baron and his friends would be under great obligations to you.

TO GOVERNOR WILLIAM LIVINGSTON, 29 AUGUST 1788
The Baron De Steuben informs me that he expects to set out this day on a visit to your legislature to endeavor to procure some arrangement respecting the place at Hackensack some time since granted to him by your state upon certain conditions. My anxiety for the Baron's situation induces me to take

the liberty of asking your friendship to him as far as may consist with considerations of propriety. It is needless to say to you that he has been a most useful servant of the public. I imagine it is as little necessary to observe, that he is a man, the qualities of whose heart entitle him to the Sympathy and good will of good men. I shall only add that he is in a condition, for a man of his temper and habits, deplorable. He is as nearly as much in debts as all the property he has *would sell for,* and he is at the same time moneyless. Congress are now discussing his last application on the footing of a contract; but there are some circumstances which involve the transaction in obscurity; and there are individuals not disposed to overcome difficulties. I fear little is to be looked for. The question, however is—Shall we permit a man, who has effectually served the American cause, either to starve or to go abroad begging?

TO ANGELICA SCHUYLER CHURCH, NEW YORK,
8 NOVEMBER 1789
The good Baron has more than ever riveted himself in my affection: to observe his unaffected solicitude and see his old eyes brimful of sympathy had something in it that won my whole soul and filled me with more than usual complacency for human nature.

TO JAMES DUANE, NEW YORK, 7 MAY 1790
The form of the bill [to compensate von Steuben] has been changed today. He is to be paid 7000 Dollars & an annuity for life but the blank is not filled up. Nobody talks of less than 1500 Dollars. The Baron says his contract or nothing; but you & all his friends must join me in telling him that to act upon this would be to act like a boy. This must be done before you leave town.

THOMAS TREDELL

TO ROBERT MORRIS, ALBANY, N.Y., 13 AUGUST 1782
Tredwell is esteemed a sensible and an honest man.

ROBERT TROUP

TO PRESIDENT GEORGE WASHINGTON, NEW YORK,
10 NOVEMBER 1796
The Legislature having appointed Mr. Laurance district Judge—a succession will of course be to be provided. A conviction of his competency, a high opinion of his worth, and a long established personal friendship induce me to take the liberty of *precipitating* a recommendation to you of Mr. *Troup,* the present Clerk of the District and Circuit court (the *Attorney* of the District being known to be disinclined to the Office). Mr. Troup is a lawyer, professionally very respectable, so that his practice is inferior in productiveness to no other—but he has by the most unexceptionable means acquired a property sufficient to make it reasonable in him to withdraw from practice upon a salary such as that of the District Judge & latterly his health has somewhat suffered from a long course of *excessive application.* His moral character is without an imputation of any sort—indeed no man in the state is better esteemed than this Gentleman. So that, I believe, the appointment would be considered as altogether fit. I trust however that in expressing myself thus strongly it will not occasion to you a moment's embarrassment, if any candidate more agreeable to you shall occur.

PIERRE VAN CORTLANDT

TO ROBERT MORRIS, ALBANY, N.Y., 13 AUGUST 1782
I omitted speaking of the Lt. Governor in his place. I shall only say he is an honest man, without pretensions.

GULIAN VERPLANK

TO OLIVER WOLCOTT, JR., ALBANY, N.Y., 22 APRIL 1797
Gulian ver Plank (now President of the Bank of New York). He is a man of superior mental endowments to any of those who have been named [as possible collector of taxes] of superior acquirements. His moral character is of the most estimable sort. His habits have not led to a familiarity with accounts—& he is supposed not much addicted to labor. But I think he would *upon principle* apply himself closely to a good execution of whatever he should undertake. He is a man of moderate fortune & has no particular pursuit—so that I think he might be willing to accept though I am not certain.

MERCY OTIS WARREN

TO MERCY OTIS WARREN, PHILADELPHIA, 1 JULY 1791
Madam,—In making you, thus late, my acknowledgements for the honor you did me, by presenting me with a volume of your poems, I dare not attempt an apology for the delay. I can only throw myself upon your clemency for a pardon.

I have not however been equally delinquent towards the work itself, which I have read, more than once, with great interest. It is certain that in the Ladies of Castille, the sex will find a new occasion of triumph. Not being a poet myself, I am in the less danger of feeling mortification at the idea, that in the career of dramatic composition at least, female genius in the United States has outstripped the Male.

GEORGE WASHINGTON

TO PRESIDENT OF CONGRESS ELIAS BOUDINOT,
NEW BRUNSWICK, N.J., 5 JULY 1778
[On Washington at the Battle of Monmouth.] As we approached the supposed place of action we heard some flying

rumors of what had happened in consequence of which the General rode forward and found the troops retiring in the greatest disorder and the enemy pressing upon their rear. I never saw the general to so much advantage. His coolness and firmness were admirable. He instantly took measures for checking the enemy's form and make a proper disposition. He then rode back and had the troops formed on a very advantageous piece of ground; in which and in other transactions of the day General Greene & Lord Stirling rendered very essential service, and did themselves great honor. The sequel is, we beat the enemy and killed and wounded at least a thousand of their best troops. America owes a great deal to General Washington for this day's work; a general rout, dismay and disgrace would have attended the whole army in any other hands but his. By his own good sense and fortitude he turned the fate of the day. Other officers have great merit in performing their parts well; but he directed the whole with the skill of a Master workman. He did not hug himself at a distance and leave an Arnold to win laurels for him;* but by his own presence, he brought order out of confusion, animated his troops and led them to success.

*A reference to General Horatio Gates and the Battle of Saratoga in September 1777.

TO PHILIP SCHUYLER, NEW WINDSOR, N.Y.,
18 FEBRUARY 1781

I always disliked the office of an Aide de Camp as having in it a kind of personal dependence. I refused to serve in this capacity with two Major Generals at an early period of the war. Infected however with the enthusiasm of the times, an idea of the General's character which experience soon taught me to be unfounded, overcame my scruples and induced me to accept his invitation to enter into his family. I believe you know the place I held in the General's confidence and councils of which will make it the more extraordinary to you to learn that for three years past I have felt no friendship for him and have professed none. The truth is our own dispositions are the opposites of each other & the pride of my temper would not suffer me to profess what I did not feel. Indeed when advances of this kind have been made to me on his part they were received in a manner that showed at least I had no inclination to court them, and that I wished to stand rather upon a footing of military confidence than of private attachment. You are too good a judge of human nature not to be sensible how this conduct in me must have operated on a man to whom all the world is offering incense. . . .

The General is a very honest man. His competitors have slender abilities and less integrity. His popularity has often been essential to the safety of America, and is still of great importance to it. These considerations have influenced my past conduct respecting him, and will influence my future. I think it is necessary he should be supported.

DEFENSE OF THE PRESIDENT'S NEUTRALITY PROCLAMATION, PHILADELPHIA, MAY 1793
[George Washington was] that man who at the head of our armies fought so successfully for the liberty and independence which are now our pride and our boast; who during the war supported the hopes, united the hearts, and nerved the arm of his countrymen; who at the close of it, unseduced by ambition and the love of power, soothed and appeased the discontents of his suffering companions in arms and with them left the proud scenes of a victorious field for the modest retreats of private life.

TO TOBIAS LEAR, NEW YORK, 2 JANUARY 1800
Your letter of the 15 of December last was delayed in getting to hand by the circumstance of its having gone to New York

while I was at Philadelphia and of its having arrived at Philadelphia after I had set out on my return to New York.

The very painful event which it announces had, previously to the receipt of it, filled my heart with bitterness. Perhaps no man in this community has equal cause with myself to deplore the loss. I have been much indebted to the kindness of the General, and he was an Aegis very essential to me. But regrets are unavailing. For great misfortunes it is the business of reason to seek consolation. The friends of General Washington have very noble ones. If virtue can secure happiness in another world he is happy. In this the Seal is now put upon his Glory. It is no longer in jeopardy from the fickleness of fortune.

P.S. In whose hands are his papers gone? Our very confidential situation will not permit this to be a point of indifference to me.

TO RUFUS KING, NEW YORK, 5 JANUARY 1800
The irreparable loss of an inestimable man removes a control [over factiousness] which was felt and was very salutary.

LETTER CONCERNING THE PUBLIC CONDUCT AND CHARACTER OF JOHN ADAMS, NEW YORK, 24 OCTOBER 1800
Very different from the practice of Mr. Adams was that of the modest and sage Washington. He consulted much, pondered much, resolved slowly, resolved surely.

JAMES WILKINSON

TO GEORGE WASHINGTON, NEW YORK, 15 JUNE 1799
I have just received a letter from General Wilkinson dated the 13 of April, in which he assures me that he will set out in the ensuing month for the seat of Government. The interview with him will be useful.

It strikes me forcibly that it will be both right and expedient

to advance this Gentleman to the grade of Major General—
He has been long steadily in service and long a Brigadier. This
in a so considerable an extension of the military establishment
gives him a pretension to promotion.

I am aware that some doubts have been entertained of him,
and that his character on certain sides gives room for doubts.
Yet he is at present in the service—is a man of more than
ordinary talent—of courage and enterprise—has discovered
upon various occasions a good zeal—has embraced military
pursuits as a profession and, will naturally find his interest as
an ambitious man in deserving the favour of the Government;
while he will be apt to become disgusted, if neglected, and
through disgust may be rendered really what he is now only
suspected to be—Under such circumstances, it seems to be
good policy to avoid all just ground of discontent and to make
it the interest of the individual to pursue his duty.

TO SECRETARY OF WAR JAMES MCHENRY, NEW YORK,
25 JUNE 1799

General Wilkinson is soon expected. I am strongly inclined to
see him made a Major General. He has now had a great deal
of experience—he possesses considerable military information—he has activity, courage and Talents. His pretensions to
promotion in every view are strong. If he should become disgusted without it, it would not be extraordinary.

Half-confidence is always bad. This officer has adopted
Military life as a profession. What can his ambition do better
than be faithful to the Government if it gives him fair play?

TO PRESIDENT JOHN ADAMS, NEW YORK,
7 SEPTEMBER 1799

General Wilkinson, who has been some weeks in the City, in
consequence of an invitation having for object the readjustment of our Western Military affairs, is about to make a journey

to *Braintree* to pay his respects to you. On such an occasion, I hope it will not be thought improper that I should address you on the subject of this officer; since what I shall say will accord with what I know to be the views of General Washington and with what I have reason to believe has been already suggested to you, with his support, by the Secretary of War [James McHenry].

You are apprised, Sir, that General Wilkinson served with distinction in our revolutionary war, and acquired in it the rank of Brigadier General—that for many years since that war he has been in the military service of the Government with the same rank, in which rank he for some time had the chief command of the army—That he has also served with distinction, in this latter period, General [Anthony] Wayne, who was not his friend, has, in one instance within my knowledge, very amply testified.

The decided impression on my mind as the result of all that I have heard or known of this Officer, is that he is eminently qualified as to talents, is brave, enterprising, active and diligent, warmly animated by the genuine spirit of his profession and devoted to it. The recent communications between us have satisfied me more than ever that he is well entitled to the character I have just given of him.

So circumstanced and so qualified, all military usage and analogy give the General a very strong claim to promotion. His sensibility would suffer with reason, if he has it not, and it would require more than usual patriotism and magnanimity to preserve him from discontent and disgust.

I, as well as others, have heard hard things said of the General, but I have never seen the shadow of proof, and I have been myself too much the victim of obloquy, to listen to detraction unsupported by facts.

Permit me to add, that I hold nothing so unsafe in public

affairs as *half confidence*—that in my opinion to employ a man in delicate and important stations, and to act towards him so as to convince him that he is not trusted and is not to receive the common share of public reward, is the most effectual way that can be adopted to make him unfaithful: while, if we only allow him a well-informed ambition, his fidelity may be assured by letting him see that it will best advance the interest of his ambition.

In hazarding these remarks, I do not mean to present to you observations which could possibly escape your own reflections; but merely to indicate the manner of viewing the subject which determines my judgment that it is both right and expedient to promote General Wilkinson to the rank of Major General in the present army. . . .

I will make no apology for the liberty I take by this letter. The solitariness of the example will I trust evince that it is not my wish to travel out of the regular and ordinary road of communication.

OLIVER WOLCOTT, JR.

TO PRESIDENT GEORGE WASHINGTON, PHILADELPHIA,
17 APRIL 1791

You will probably recollect that previous to your departure from this place, anticipating the event which has taken place with regard to the death of Mr. Eveleigh, I took the liberty to mention to you that Mr. Wolcott the present Auditor would be in every respect worthy of your consideration as his successor in office.

Now that the event has happened, a concern as anxious as it is natural for the success of the department united with a sentiment of Justice towards Mr. Wolcott leads me to a repetition of that Idea. This Gentleman's conduct in the station he now fills has been that of an excellent officer. It has not only been good but distinguished. It has combined all the requisites which could be desired; moderation with firmness, liberality with exactness, indefatigable industry with an accurate & sound discernment a thorough knowledge of business & a remarkable spirit of order & arrangement. Indeed I ought to say that I owe very much of whatever success may have attended the merely executive operation of the department to Mr. Wolcott. And I do not fear to commit myself, when I add, that he possesses in an eminent degree all the qualifications desirable in a Comptroller of the Treasury—that it is scarcely possible to find a man in the United States more competent to the duties of that station than himself, *few* who would be equally so. It may truly be said of him that he is a man of *rare* merit. And I have good evidence that he has been viewed in this light by the members of Congress extensively from different quarters of the Union, and is so considered by all that part of the public, who have had opportunities of witnessing his conduct.

The immediate relation too, which his present situation bears to that of Comptroller is a strong argument in his favor. Though a regular gradation of office is not admissible in a strict sense in regard to offices of a civil nature and is wholly inapplicable to those of the first rank (such as the heads of the great executive departments) yet a certain regard to the relation, which one situation bears to another is consonant with natural ideas of Justice and is recommended by powerful considerations of policy. . . .

In addition to the rest, Mr. Wolcott's experience, in this particular line, pleads powerfully in his favor. This experience may be dated back to his office of Comptroller of the State of Connecticut and has been perfected by practice in his present place.

A question may perhaps Sir arise in your mind whether some inconvenience may not attend his removal from his present office. I am of opinion that no sensible inconvenience will be felt on this score; since it will be easy for him as Comptroller, who is the immediate superior of the auditor to form any man of business for the office he will leave in a short period time. More inconvenience would be felt by the introduction of a Comptroller, not in the immediate train of the business. Besides this it may be observed that a degree of inconvenience on this score cannot be deemed an obstacle, but upon a principle which would bar the progress of merit from one station to another. On this point of inconvenience a reflection occurs which I do not think I ought to suppress. Mr. Wolcott is a man of nice sensibility, not unconscious of his own value; and he doubtless must believe that he has pretensions from situation to the Office. Should another appointment take place & he resign, the derangement of the department would truly be distressing to the public service.

In suggesting thus particularly the reasons which in my mind operate in favor of Mr. Wolcott, I am influenced by information that other characters will be brought to your view by weighty advocates, and as I think it more than possible that Mr. Wolcott may not be mentioned to you by any other person than myself, I feel it a duty arising out of my situation in the department to bear my full & explicit testimony to his worth; confident that he will justify by every kind of *substantial* merit any mark of your approbation, which he may receive.

TO DUTCH BANKERS, TREASURY DEPARTMENT,
PHILADELPHIA, 31 JANUARY 1795

The Gentleman whom The President has determined to nominate as my Successor and who will be no doubt appointed is Oliver Wolcott Esquire the present Comptroller of the Treasury. I do him no more than Justice, by assuring you, that he is a Gentleman of undoubted intelligence, probity and good principles with regard to Public Credit. The confidence of yourselves and your Countrymen may be safely reposed in him.

TO OLIVER WOLCOTT, JR., NEW YORK, 5 APRIL 1797
I hope nothing in my last was misunderstood. Could it be necessary, I would assure you that no one has a stronger conviction than myself, of the purity of the motives which direct your public conduct, or of the good sense and judgment by which it is guided. If I have a fear (you will excuse my frankness) it is, lest the strength of your feelings, the companion of energy of character, should prevent that pliancy to circumstances which is sometimes indispensable. I beg you only to watch yourself on this score, and the public will always find in you an able, as well as faithful servant.

ABRAHAM YATES, JR.

TO SUPERINTENDENT OF FINANCE ROBERT MORRIS, ALBANY, N.Y., 13 AUGUST 1782
[Mr. Yates] is a man whose ignorance and perverseness are only surpassed by his pertinacity and conceit. He hates all highflyers, which is the appellation he gives to men of genius. He has the merit of being always the first man at the [state] Legislature. The people have been a long time in the *habit* of choosing him in different offices; and to the title of prescription, he adds that of being a preacher to their taste. He *assures* them, they are too poor to pay taxes. He is a staunch whig, that deserves to be pensioned by the British Ministry. He is commissioner of the loan office in this state.

ROBERT YATES

TO SUPERINTENDENT OF FINANCE ROBERT MORRIS,
ALBANY, N.Y., 13 AUGUST 1782
Judge Yates is upright and respectable in his profession.

TO THE SUPERVISORS OF THE CITY OF ALBANY,
NEW YORK, 18 FEBRUARY 1789
[Explaining why Federalists selected Robert Yates, an Antifederalist, as their candidate to run against Governor George Clinton in the 1789 gubernatorial election.] It appeared therefore most advisable to select some man of the opposite party, to whose integrity, patriotism and temper, confidence might justly be placed, however little his political opinions on the question lately agitated, might be approved by those who were assembled upon the occasion.

Among the persons of this description, there were circumstances which led to a decision in favor of Judge Yates. And we flatter ourselves that this decision, to those who are acquainted with the situation of the state, will be most likely to appear well founded. It is certain, that as a man and a judge, he is generally esteemed. And though his opposition to the new constitution was such as its friends cannot but disapprove; yet since the period of its adoption, his conduct has been tempered with a degree of moderation and regard to peace and decorum which entitle him to credit; and seem to point him out as a man likely to compose the differences of the state, and to unite its citizens in the harmonious pursuit of their common and genuine interest.

Of this at least we feel confident, that he has no personal revenge to gratify, no opponents to oppress, no partisans to provide for, nor any promises for personal purposes to be performed at the public expence. On the contrary we trust he will be found to be a man who looks with an equal eye on his fellow citizens, and who will be more ambitious of leaving a good name, than a good estate, to his posterity.

TO THE ELECTORS OF THE STATE OF NEW YORK,
NEW YORK, 7 APRIL 1789
Judge Yates is now a popular character, and it will not be doubted that he is a man of sense and integrity.

Emblematic Quotations

ADDRESS AND STRATEGY

Where force failed, address and strategem still won the prize.
Eulogy on Nathanael Greene, New York,
4 July 1789

ADMINISTRATION

Though we cannot acquiesce in the political heresy of the poet who says—

"For forms of government let fools contest—
That which is best administered is best."*

Yet we may safely pronounce that the true test of a good government is its aptitude and tendency to produce a good administration.

*Alexander Pope, *Essay on Man.*
The Federalist No. 68, New York
Independent Journal, 12 March 1788

ADVERSITY

I am aware that a man of real merit is never seen in so favorable a light as through the medium of adversity. The clouds that surround him are shades that set off his good qualities. Misfortune cuts down the little vanities that in prosperous times served as so many spots in his virtues and gives a tone of humility that makes his worth more amiable.
To John Laurens, Preakness, N.J., 11 October 1780

AMBITION

Great ambition unchecked by principle or the love of glory, is an unruly tyrant which never can keep long in a course which good men will approve.
To James A. Bayard, New York, 16 January 1801

APPEARANCES

In a popular Government *appearances* are a good deal.
To Jonathan Dayton, New York, 30 March 1798

ARGUMENTATION

To overrate the value or force of our own arguments is a natural foible of self-love—to be convinced without convincing others is no uncommon fate of a writer or speaker.
*The Defence No. XXII, New York,
5–11 November 1795*

BAD MEN

Bad men are apt to paint others like themselves.
A Full Vindication of the Measures of Congress, &c., New York, 15 December 1774

BOLDNESS

Success was answerable to the judicious boldness of the design.
*Eulogy on Nathanael Greene, New York,
4 July 1789*

BREVITY

In all military documents it is peculiarly desirable to consult conciseness as far as it may comport with perspicuity and accuracy. Military men in the midst of active operations have very little leisure for writing.

To Caleb Swan, New York, 22 September 1799

CHRISTIAN FORTITUDE

We live in a world full of evil. In the latter period of life misfortunes sent to thicken round us, and our duty and our peace both require that we should accustom ourselves to meet disasters with Christian fortitude.

*To Elizabeth Hamilton, New York,
16–17 March 1803*

COMMERCE

An active commerce, an extensive navigation, and a flourishing marine would then be the inevitable offspring of moral and physical necessity. We might defy the little arts of little politicians to control, or vary, the irresistible and unchangeable course of nature.

*The Federalist No. 11, New York
Independent Journal, 24 November 1787*

CONFORMITY

Men are fond of going with the stream.

To James Wilson, New York, 25 January 1789

CONSTITUTION MAKING

We must bear in mind, that we are not to confine our view to the present period, but to look forward to remote futurity. Constitutions of civil Government are not to be framed upon a calculation of existing exigencies; but upon a combination of these, with the probable exigencies of ages, according to the natural and tried course of human affairs. Nothing therefore can be more fallacious, than to infer the extent of any power, proper to be lodged in the National Government, from an estimate of its immediate necessities. There ought to be a CAPACITY to provide for future contingencies, as they may happen; and, as these are illimitable in their nature, it is impossible safely to limit that capacity.

The Federalist No. 34, New York Independent Journal, 5 January 1788

CONTROLLING EVENTS

The best way is ever not to attempt to stem a torrent but to divert it.

To George Washington, Philadelphia, 17 March 1783

DECEPTION

Mankind are forever destined to be the dupes of bold and cunning imposture.

To Charles Cotesworth Pinckney, New York, 29 December 1802

DEFERENCE

I am not one of those who gain an influence by cajoling the unthinking mass (tho' I pity their delusions) and ringing in their ears the gracious sound of their *absolute Sovereignty*. I despise the trick of such dirty policy. I know there are Citizens, who, to gain their own private ends, enflame the minds of the well meaning, tho' less intelligent parts of the community, by sating their vanity with that cordial and unfailing specific, that all power is seated in the People. For my part, I am not much attached to the Majesty of the multitude, and therefore wave all pretentions (founded on such conduct) to their countenance. I consider them in general as very ill qualified to judge for themselves what government will best suit their peculiar situations; nor is this to be wondered at—the science of Government is not easily understood. . . . When a new form of Government is fabricated, it lies with the people at large to receive or reject it:—this is their *inherent right.* Now, I would ask, (without intending to triumph over the weaknesses or follies of any men) how are the people to profit by this inherent right? By what conduct do they discover, that they are sensible of their own interest in this situation? Is it by the exercise of a well disciplined reason, and a correspondent education? I believe not. How then? As I humbly conceive, by a tractable and docile disposition, and by honest men endeavoring to keep their minds easy; while others, of the same disposition, with the advantages of genius and learning, are constructing the bark that may, by the blessing of Heaven, carry them to the port of rest and happiness; if they will embark without dissidence, and proceed without mutiny. I know this is blunt and ungracious reasoning: it is the best, however, which I am prepared to offer on this momentous business; and, since my own heart does not reproach me, I shall not be very solicitous about its reception. If truth, then, is permitted to speak, the mass of the people of America (any more than the mass of other countries) cannot judge with any degree of precision concerning the fitness of the New Constitution to the peculiar situation of America:—they have, however, done wisely in delegating the power of framing a Government to those every way worthy and well qualified; and, if this Government is snatched, untasted from them, it may not be amiss to enquire into the causes which will probably occasion their disappointment.

Cæsar No. II, New York Daily Advertiser,
17 October 1787

DEMAGOGUES

There are always men in society of some talents, but more ambition, in quest of *that* which it would be impossible for them to obtain in any other way than by working on the passions and prejudices of the less discerning classes of citizens and yeomanry.—It is the plan of men of this stamp to frighten the people with ideal bugbears, in order to mould them to their own purposes. The unceasing cry of these designing croakers is, my friends, your liberty is invaded! Have you thrown off the yoke of one tyrant, to invest yourselves with that of another! Have you fought, bled, and conquered, for *such a change!* If you have—go—retire into silent obscurity, and kiss the rod that scourges you.

Cæsar No. II, New York Daily Advertiser,
17 October 1787

DISCRETION

A prudent silence will frequently be taken for wisdom, and a sentence or two cautiously thrown in will sometimes gain the palm of knowledge, while a man well informed but indiscreet and unreserved will not uncommonly talk himself out of all consideration and weight.

> To James A. Hamilton, New York, June 1804

Discretion is the MENTOR which ought to accompany every Young *Telemachus* in his journey through life.

> To James A. Hamilton, New York, June 1804

DIVIDE AND CONQUER

Divide et impera must be the motto of every nation, that either hates or fears us.

> The Federalist No. 7, New York
> Independent Journal, 17 November 1787

DOING WHAT IS RIGHT

The real failure to do right . . . often sinks the government as well as individuals into merited contempt.

> The Defence of the Funding System,
> New York, July 1795

Let us be Right, because to do right is intrinsically proper and I verily believe it is the best means of securing final success.

> To Rufus King, New York, 13 April 1796

DUTY

'Tis a good old maxim to which we may safely adhere in most cases that we ought to do our duty and leave the rest to the care of heaven.

> To William Gordon, West Point, N.Y.,
> 5 September 1779

ELECTIONS

The natural cure for an ill administration, in a popular or representative constitution, is a change of men.
The Federalist No. 21, New York
Independent Journal, 12 December 1787

EMERGENCIES

Emergencies . . . will sometimes arise in all societies, however constituted; that seditions and insurrections are unhappily maladies as inseparable from the body politic, as tumours and eruptions from the natural body; that the idea of governing at all times by the simple force of law (which we have been told is the only admissible principle of republican government) has no place but in the reveries of those political doctors, whose sagacity disdains the admonitions of experimental instruction.
The Federalist No. 28, New York
Independent Journal, 26 December 1787

In emergencies great and difficult, not to act with an energy proportioned to their magnitude and pressure is as dangerous as any other conceivable course.
Edmund Randolph (drafted by Hamilton) to
Governor Thomas Mifflin, Philadelphia,
7 August 1794

In an emergency like the present, energy is wisdom.
To Charles Cotesworth Pinckney, New York,
29 December 1802

ENEMIES

There is no greater error than that of undervaluing an enemy, but with one exception, which is that of overvaluing them.
To Robert R. Livingston, Germantown, Pa.,
7 August 1777

No man is without his personal enemies. Pre-eminence even in talents and virtue is a cause of envy and hatred of its possessor. Bad men are the natural enemies of virtuous men. Good men sometimes mistake and dislike each other.
The Defence No. 1, New York, 22 July 1795

EXAMPLE

There is a contagion in example which few men have sufficient force of mind to resist.
The Federalist No. 61, New York Packet,
26 February 1788

EXAGGERATIONS

To embellish military exploits, and varnish military disgraces, is no unusual policy.
"H.G." Letter No. 2, New York Daily Advertiser, *11 March 1789*

EXCISE TAXES

The genius of the people will ill brook the inquisitive and peremptory spirit of excise laws.
The Federalist No. 12, New York Packet,
27 November 1787

EXECUTIVE POWER

It is of the nature of war to increase the executive at the expence of the legislative authority.

The Federalist No. 8, New York Packet,
20 November 1787

There is an idea, which is not without its advocates, that a vigorous executive is inconsistent with the genius of republican government. The enlightened well wishers to this species of government must at least hope that the supposition is destitute of foundation; since they can never admit its truth, without at the same time admitting the condemnation of their own principles. Energy in the executive is a leading character in the definition of good government. It is essential to the protection of the community against foreign attacks: It is not less essential to the steady administration of the laws, to the protection of property against those irregular and high handed combinations, which sometimes interrupt the ordinary course of justice, to the security of liberty against the enterprises and assaults of ambition, of faction and of anarchy. . . .

A feeble executive implies a feeble execution of the government. A feeble execution is but another phrase for a bad execution: And a government ill executed, whatever it may be in theory, must be in practice a bad government.

The Federalist No. 70, New York
Independent Journal, 15 March 1788

EXPERIENCE

The best oracle of wisdom, experience.

The Federalist No. 15, New York
Independent Journal, 1 December 1787

FACTIONS

It ought not to be forgotten, that the demon of faction will at certain seasons extend his scepter over all numerous bodies of men.

The Federalist No. 65, New York Packet,
7 March 1788

FALSE INFORMATION

How apt a spirit of ill-informed jealousy, or of too great abstraction and refinement is to lead men astray from the plainest paths of reason and conviction.

The Federalist No. 17, New York Packet,
27 November 1787

FEDERALISM

It may be said, that it would tend to render the government of the Union too powerful, and to enable it to absorb in itself those residicary authorities, which it might be judged proper to leave with the States for local purposes. Allowing the utmost latitude to the love of power, which any reasonable man can require, I confess I am at a loss to discover what temptation the persons entrusted with the administration of the general government could ever feel to divest the States of the authorities of that description. . . . It will always be far more easy for the State governments to encroach upon the national authorities, than for the national government to encroach upon the State authorities.

The Federalist No. 17, New York
Independent Journal, 5 December 1787

An intire consolidation of the States into one complete national sovereignty would imply an intire subordination of the parts; and whatever powers might remain in them would be altogether dependent on the general will. But as the plan of the Convention aims only at a partial Union or consolidation, the State Governments would clearly retain all the rights of sovereignty which they before had and which were not by that act *exclusively* delegated to the United States.

> *The Federalist No. 31, New York*
> Independent Journal, *2 January 1788*

If the Fœderal Government should overpass the just bounds of its authority, and make a tyrannical use of its powers; the people whose creature it is must appeal to the standard they have formed, and take such measures to redress the injury done to the constitution, as the exigency may suggest and prudence justify.

> *The Federalist No. 31, New York*
> Independent Journal, *8 January 1788*

FINDING A HUSBAND

Get a man of sense, not ugly enough to be pointed at, with some good-nature, a few grains of feeling, a little taste, a little imagination, and above all a good deal of decision to keep you in order, for that I foresee will be no easy task. If you can find one with all these qualities willing to marry you, marry him as soon as you please.

> *To Margarita Schuyler, New Windsor, N.Y.,*
> *21 January 1783*

FINDING A WIFE

She must be young, handsome (I lay most stress upon a good shape) sensible (a little learning will do), well bred (but she must have an aversion to the word ton), chaste and tender (I am an enthusiast in my notions of fidelity and fondness), of some good nature, a great deal of generosity (she must neither love money nor scolding, for I dislike equally a termagant and an economist). In politics, I am indifferent what side she may be of; I think I have arguments that will easily convert her to mine. As to religion, a moderate stock will satisfy me. She must believe in God and hate a saint. But as to fortune, the larger stock of that the better.

To John Laurens, Middlebrook, N.J., April 1779

FIRMNESS

Real firmness is good for every thing. *Strut* is good for nothing.

To Oliver Wolcott, Jr., New York, 6 June 1797

FIRST PRINCIPLES

In disquisitions of every kind there are certain primary truths or first principles upon which all subsequent reasonings must depend. These contain an internal evidence, which antecedent to all reflection or combination commands the assent of the mind.

The Federalist No. 30, New York Packet, 1 January 1788

FRANCE

There is no country I have a greater curiosity to see or which I am persuaded would be so interesting to me as yours.

To Vicomte de Noailles, April-June 1782

I did not fight against G B to obtain Independence merely for the pleasure of surrendering it to France. I am ready to risk every thing on its support.

To Jonathan Dayton, New York, 15 March 1798

GAMBLING

Gambling, a vice destructive to the reputation of an army, and fraught with every evil not only to those who suffer themselves to engage in it, but to the army in which it is tolerated, is strictly prohibited.

General Orders, New York, 10 January 1800

GENERAL SURMISES

General surmises never lead to the discovery of truth.

Speech in the New York Ratifying Convention,
28 June 1788

GOOD WITH THE BAD

No wise statesman will reject the good from an apprehension of the ill. The truth is in human affairs there is no good, pure and unmixed; every advantage has two sides, and wisdom consists in availing ourselves of the good and guarding as much as possible against the bad.

To Robert Morris, DePeyster's Point, N.Y.,
30 April 1781

'Tis the lot of every thing human to mingle a portion of ill with the good.

To Rufus King, Philadelphia, 8 July 1791

GOSSIP

[Alluding to a reference to Madison insinuating "unfavourable impressions of me."] I suspended my opinion on the subject. I knew the malevolent officiousness of mankind too well to yield a very ready acquiescence to the suggestions which were made, and resolved to wait 'till time and more experience should afford a solution.

To Edward Carrington, Philadelphia,
26 May 1792

I have never seen the shadow of proof, and I have been myself too much the victim of obloquy, to listen to detraction unsupported by facts.

To President John Adams, New York,
7 September 1799

GOVERNMENT

Why has government been instituted at all? Because the passions of men will not conform to the dictates of reason and justice, without constraint.

The Federalist No. 15, New York Independent Journal, *1 December 1787*

I believe it may be regarded as a position, warranted by the history of mankind, that in the usual progress of things, the necessities of a nation *in every stage of its existence will be found at least equal to its resources.*

The Federalist No. 30, New York Packet,
28 December 1787

A government ought to contain in itself every power requisite to the full accomplishment of the objects committed to its care, and to the complete execution of the trusts for which it is responsible; free from every other control, but a regard to the public good and to the sense of the people.

The Federalist No. 30, New York Packet,
1 January 1788

If mankind were to resolve to agree in no institution of government, until every part of it had been adjusted to the most exact standard of perfection, society would soon become a general scene of anarchy, and the world a desert.

The Federalist No. 65, New York Packet,
7 March 1788

HALF-CONFIDENCE

I hold nothing so unsafe in public affairs as *half confidence*—that in my opinion to employ a man in delicate and important stations, and to act towards him so as to convince him that he is not trusted and is not to receive the common share of public reward, is the most effectual way that can be adopted to make him unfaithful: while, if we only allow him a well-informed ambition, his fidelity may be assured by letting him see that it will best advance the interest of his ambition.

To President John Adams, New York,
7 September 1799

HAPPINESS

Experience more and more convinces me that true happiness is only to be found in the bosom of one's own family.

To Elizabeth Hamilton, Albany, N.Y.,
25 October 1801

HARSH WORDS

Harsh words are very rarely useful in public proceedings.
To Oliver Wolcott, Jr., New York, 6 June 1797

HONESTY

One great error is that we suppose mankind more honest than they are.
Speech in the Constitutional Convention, Philadelphia, 22 June 1787

HONOR

True honor is a rational thing. It is as distinguishable from Quixotism as true courage from the spirit of a bravo.
The Defence No V, New York, 5 August 1795

HUMAN NATURE

The safest reliance of every government is on men's interests. This is a principle of human nature on which all political speculation, to be just, must be founded.
A Letter from Phocion to the Considerate Citizens of New York, New York, 1–27 January 1784

Men are ambitious, vindictive and rapacious.
The Federalist No. 6, New York Independent Journal, 14 November 1787

Is it not time to awake from the deceitful dream of a golden age, and to adopt as a practical maxim for the direction of our political conduct, that we, as well as the other inhabitants of the globe, are yet remote from the happy empire of perfect wisdom and perfect virtue?

The Federalist No. 6, New York
Independent Journal, 14 November 1787

The supposition of universal venality in human nature is little less an error in political reasoning than the supposition of universal rectitude.

The Federalist No. 76, New York Packet,
1 April 1788

It may seem strange to some, that a man who had behaved well in one situation should be so entirely defective or faulty in another. But when acquainted with human nature and its history on a large scale, [anyone] will be sensible that there is nothing extraordinary in the thing. Many of those who have proved the worst scourges of society have, in the commencement of their career, been its brightest ornaments. These fair beginnings are sometimes the effect of premeditation to pave the way to future mischief: at other times, they are the natural result of a mixed character placed in favorable circumstances.

"H.G." Letter IV, New York Daily Advertiser,
14 March 1789

IMAGINATION

Imagination may range at pleasure till it gets bewildered amidst the labyrinths of an enchanted castle, and knows not on which side to turn to extricate itself from the perplexities into which it has so rashly adventured.

The Federalist No. 30, New York Packet,
1 January 1788

IMMIGRATION

If lenity and moderation are observed in administering the laws, the natural advantages of this fertile infant country, united to the indulgence given to their religion, will attract droves of emigrants from all the Roman Catholic States in Europe, and these colonies, in time, will themselves be encompassed with innumerable hosts of neighbors, disaffected to them, both because of difference in religion and government. How dangerous their situation would be, let every man of common-sense judge.
Remarks on the Quebec Bill, 22 June 1775

INDIFFERENCE

I condemn those indifferent mortals, who either never form opinions, or never make them known.
*Speech in the New York Ratifying Convention,
28 June 1788*

INDUSTRY AND FRUGALITY

Cultivate also industry and frugality. They are auxiliaries of good morals and great sources of private and national prosperity.
*Draft of Washington's Farewell Address,
30 July 1796*

INGENUITY

Ingenious men may say ingenious things.
*Speech in the New York Ratifying Convention,
28 June 1788*

INITIATIVE

In Politics as in war the first blow is half the battle.
To Isaac Ledyard, Jamaica, N.Y., 18 February 1789

INTOLERANCE

There is bigotry in politics, as well as in religions, equally pernicious in both. The zealots of either description are ignorant of the advantage of a spirit of toleration.
Second Letter from Phocion . . . ,
New York, April 1784

INTRIGUE

Nothing was more to be desired, than that every practicable obstacle should be opposed to cabal, intrigue and corruption. These most deadly adversaries of republican government might naturally have been expected to make their approaches from more than one quarter.
The Federalist No. 68, New York
Independent Journal, 12 March 1788

Talents for low intrigue and the little arts of popularity may alone suffice to elevate a man to the first honors in a single state; but it will require other talents and a different kind of merit to establish him in the esteem and confidence of the whole union, or of so considerable a portion of it as would be necessary to make him a successful candidate for the distinguished office of president of the United States.
The Federalist No. 68, New York
Independent Journal, 12 March 1788

JEALOUSY

Jealousy is a predominant passion of human nature and is a source of the greatest evils.

"A Sincere Friend to America," The Farmer Refuted &c., New York, 23 February 1775

JUDICIARY

The majesty of the national authority must be manifested through the medium of the Courts of Justice.

The Federalist No. 16, New York Packet, 4 December 1787

LABOR

We labor less now than any civilized nation of Europe, and a habit of labor in the people is as essential to the health and vigor of their minds and bodies as it is conducive to the welfare of the state.

To Robert Morris, DePeyster's Point, N.Y., 30 April 1781

LAWS

Government implies the power of making laws. It is essential to the idea of law, that it be attended with a sanction; or, in other words, a penalty or punishment for disobedience. If there be no penalty annexed to disobedience, the resolutions or commands which pretend to be laws will in fact amount to nothing more than advice or recommendation.

The Federalist No. 15, New York Independent Journal, 1 December 1787

LEADERSHIP

When occasions present themselves in which the interests of the people are at variance with their inclinations, it is the duty of the persons whom they have appointed to be the guardians of those interests, to withstand the temporary delusion, in order to give them time and opportunity for more cool and sedate reflection. Instances might be cited, in which a conduct of this kind has saved the people from very fatal consequences of their own mistakes, and has procured lasting monuments of their gratitude to the men, who had courage and magnanimity enough to serve them at their displeasure.

The Federalist No. 71, New York Packet,
18 March 1788

LIBERTY

There is a certain enthusiasm in liberty that makes human nature rise above itself in acts of bravery and heroism.

"A Sincere Friend to America," The Farmer
Refuted &c., *New York, 23 February 1775*

LOVE

'Tis a very good thing when their stars unite two people who are fit for each other, who have souls capable of relishing the sweets of friendship and sensibilities.

To Margarita Schuyler, New Windsor, N.Y.,
21 January 1781

MERIT

One of the best and most useful feelings of the human heart [is] a reverence for merit.

> Defense of the President's Neutrality
> Proclamation, *Philadelphia, May 1793*

MILITARY TRAINING

A tolerable expertness in military movements is a business that requires time and practice. It is not a day or even a week that will suffice for the attainment of it.

> *The Federalist No. 35, New York
> Independent Journal, 9 January 1788*

MISCHIEF

There never was any mischief but had a *priest* or a woman at the bottom.

> To John Laurens, *New York, 11 September 1779*

Men bent upon mischief are more active in the pursuit of their object than those who aim at doing good.

> A Letter from Phocion . . . ,
> *New York, 1–27 January 1784*

MISTAKES

In common life to retract an error, even in the beginning, is no easy task. Perseverance confirms us in it and rivets the difficulty; but in a public station, to have been in an error and to have persisted in it when it is detected, ruins both reputation and fortune. To this we may add that disappointment and opposition inflame the minds of men and attach them still more to their mistakes.

A Full Vindication of the Members of Congress &c., New York, 15 December 1774

MODERATION

One may as well preach moderation to the winds as to our zealots.

To Henry Lee, Philadelphia, 22 June 1793

Moderation in every nation is a virtue.

The Warning No. III, Gazette of the United States, 21 February 1797

MONEY

I hate money making men.

To John Laurens, Middlebrook, N.J., 22 May 1779

Contempt and neglect must attend those who manifest that they have no principle but to get money.

To Philip Livingston, Philadelphia, 2 April 1792

NATIONAL GOVERNMENT FOR AMERICA

There is something noble and magnificent in the perspective of a great Federal Republic, closely linked in the pursuit of a common interest, tranquil and prosperous at home, respectable abroad; but there is something proportionably diminutive and contemptible in the prospect of a number of petty States, with the appearance only of union, jarring, jealous, and perverse, without any determined direction, fluctuating and unhappy at home, weak and insignificant by their dissensions in the eyes of other nations.

Happy America, if those to whom thou hast intrusted the guardianship of thy infancy know how to provide for thy future repose, but miserable and undone, if their negligence or ignorance permits the spirit of discord to erect her banner on the ruins of thy tranquillity!

The Continentalist No. VI, New York Packet,
4 July 1782

NATIONAL SECURITY

Safety from external danger is the most powerful director of national conduct. Even the ardent love of liberty will, after a time, give way to its dictates. The violent destruction of life and property incident to war—the continual effort and alarm attendant on a state of continual danger, will compel nations the most attached to liberty, to resort for repose and security, to institutions, which have a tendency to destroy their civil and political rights. To be more safe they, at length, become willing to run the risk of being less free.

The Federalist No. 8, New York Packet,
20 November 1787

It must be admitted, as a necessary consequence, that there can be no limitation of that authority, which is to provide for the defence and protection of the community, in any matter essential to its efficacy; that is, in any matter essential to the *formation, direction* or *support* of the NATIONAL FORCES.

The Federalist No. 23, New York
Independent Journal, *18 December 1787*

To judge from the history of mankind, we shall be compelled to conclude, that the fiery and destructive passions of war, reign in the human breast, with much more powerful sway, than the mild and beneficent sentiments of peace; and, that to model our political systems upon speculations of lasting tranquility, is to calculate on the weaker springs of the human character.
The Federalist No. 34, New York Independent Journal, 5 January 1788

NEGLECTS AND SLIGHTS

Neglects and slights calculated to lessen the opinion of the importance of a thing and bring it into discredit are often the most successful weapons by which it can be attacked.
"H.G." Letter XII, New York, 8 March 1789

NEUTRALITY

The rights of neutrality will only be respected, when they are defended by an adequate power. A nation, despicable by its weakness, forfeits even the privilege of being neutral.
The Federalist No. 11, New York Independent Journal, 24 November 1787

OBSTINACY

Caution and investigation are a necessary armour against error and imposition. But this untractableness may be carried too far, and may degenerate into obstinacy, perverseness or disingenuity.
The Federalist No. 30, New York Packet, 1 January 1788

OFFICEHOLDERS

Nothing is more natural to men in office, than to look with peculiar deference towards that authority to which they owe their official existence.
The Federalist No. 22, New York Packet,
14 December 1787

OVERLOOKING FAULTS

There may often be good reasons for *overlooking* a fault which we *perceive*. To *overlook* is very different from *not to see* or not to attend to.
To James McHenry, New York, 5 August 1799

PASSION

Has it not ... invariably been found, that momentary passions and immediate interests have a more active and imperious controul over human conduct than general or remote considerations of policy, utility or justice?
The Federalist No. 6, New York
Independent Journal, 14 November 1787

Men easily heat their imaginations when their passions are heated.
To Edward Carrington, Philadelphia, 26 May 1792

Passion wrests the helm from reason.
To Rufus King, New York, 5 January 1800

Men are reasoning rather than reasonable animals, for the most part governed by the impulse of passion.
To James A. Bayard, New York, 16–21 April 1802

POLITICAL MOBILITY

There are strong minds in every walk of life that will rise superior to the disadvantages of situation, and will command the tribute due to their merit, not only from the classes to which they particularly belong, but from the society in general. The door ought to be equally open to all; and I trust, for the credit of human nature, that we shall see examples of such vigorous plants flourishing in the soil of Fœderal, as well as of State Legislation.
The Federalist No. 36, New York Packet,
8 January 1788

In those great revolutions which occasionally convulse society, human nature never fails to be brought forward in its brightest as well as in its blackest colors: And it has very properly been ranked not among the least of the advantages which compensate for the evils they produce, that they serve to bring to light talents and virtues which might otherwise have languished in obscurity or only shot forth a few scattered and wandering rays.
Eulogy on Nathanael Greene, New York,
4 July 1789

POLITICAL PARTIES

The spirit of party, in different degrees, must be expected to infect all political bodies.
The Federalist No. 26, New York
Independent Journal, 22 December 1787

POWER

History is full of examples where, in contests for liberty, a jealousy of power has either defeated the attempts to recover or perceive it, in the first instance, or has afterward subverted it by clogging government with too great precautions for its felicity, or by leaving too wide a door for sedition and popular licentiousness. In a government framed for durable liberty, not less regard must be paid to giving the magistrate a proper degree of authority to make and execute the laws with rigor, than to guard against encroachments upon the rights of the community. As too much power leads to despotism, too little leads to anarchy, and both, eventually to the ruin of the people.
The Continentalist No. 1, New York Packet,
12 July 1781

Congress ... is no doubt chargeable with mistakes, but perhaps its greatest has been too much readiness to make concessions of the powers implied in its original trust.
The Continentalist No. 3, New York Packet,
12 August 1781

An enlightened zeal for the energy and efficiency of government will be stigmatized, as the off-spring of a temper fond of despotic power and hostile to the principles of liberty. An overscrupulous jealousy of danger to the rights of the people, which is more commonly the fault of the head than of the heart, will be represented as mere pretence and artifice; the bait for popularity at the expence of public good. It will be forgotten, on the one hand, that jealousy is the usual concomitant of violent love, and that the noble enthusiasm of liberty is too apt to be infected with a spirit of narrow and illiberal distrust. On the other hand, it will be equally forgotten, that the vigour of government is essential to the security of liberty; that, in the contemplation of a sound and well informed judgment, their interest can never be separated; and that a dangerous ambition more often lurks behind the specious mask of zeal for the rights of the people, than under the forbidding appearance of zeal for the firmness and efficiency of government.

The Federalist No. 1, New York
Independent Journal, *27 October 1787*

Power controuled or abused is almost always the rival and enemy of that power by which it is controuled or abridged.

The Federalist No. 15, New York
Independent Journal, *1 December 1787*

The *means* ought to be proportioned to the *end*; the persons, from whose agency the attainment of any *end* is expected, ought to possess the *means* by which it is to be attained.

The Federalist No. 23, New York Packet,
18 December 1787

Confidence must be placed some where; that the necessity of doing it is implied in the very act of delegating power; and that it is better to hazard the abuse of that confidence, than to embarrass the government and endanger the public safety, by impolitic restrictions on the Legislative authority. . . . The citizens of America have too much discernment to be argued into anarchy. And I am much mistaken if experience has not wrought a deep and solemn conviction in the public mind, that greater energy of government is essential to the welfare and prosperity of the community.

The Federalist No. 26, New York
Independent Journal, *22 December 1787*

PROMOTION

The expectation of promotion in civil as in military life is a great stimulus to virtuous exertion: While examples of unrewarded exertion, supported by talent & qualification, are proportionable discouragements. Where they do not produce resignations, they leave men dissatisfied & a dissatisfied man seldom does his duty well.

In a government like ours, where pecuniary compensations are moderate, the principle of gradual advancement, as a reward for good conduct, is perhaps more necessary to be attended to than in others where offices are more lucrative. By due attention to it, it will operate as a means to secure respectable men for offices of inferior emolument and consequence.

To President George Washington, Philadelphia,
17 April 1791

PUBLIC ESTEEM

One of the strongest incentives to public virtue is the expectation of public esteem.

Defense of the President's Neutrality
Proclamation, Philadelphia, May 1793

PUBLIC OPINION

I approve extremely the idea of leading the public opinion. I wish all our friends to act on this ground & to take the "*air imposant.*"

To Jonathan Dayton, New York, 30 March 1798

RESPONSIBILITY IN OFFICE

Responsibility is of two kinds, to censure and to punishment. The first is the most important of the two; especially in an elective office. Man, in public trust, will much oftener act in such a manner as to render him unworthy of being any longer trusted, than in such a manner as to make him obnoxious to legal punishment. But the multiplication of the executive adds to the difficulty of detection in either case. It often becomes impossible, amidst mutual accusations, to determine on whom the blame or the punishment of a pernicious measure, or series of pernicious measures ought really to fall. It is shifted from one to another with so much dexterity, and under such plausible appearances, that the public opinion is left in suspense about the real author. The circumstances which may have led to any national miscarriage or misfortune are sometimes so complicated, that where there are a number of actors who may have had different degrees and kinds of agency, though we may clearly see upon the whole that there has been mismanagement, yet it may be impracticable to pronounce to whose account the evil which may have been incurred is truly chargeable.

The Federalist No. 70, New York Independent Journal, 15 March 1788

REVENUE

Money is with propriety considered as the vital principle of the body politic; as that which sustains its life and motion, and enables it to perform its most essential functions. A complete power therefore to procure a regular and adequate supply of it, as far as the resources of the community will permit,

may be regarded as an indispensable ingredient in every constitution.
The Federalist No. 30, New York Packet,
28 December 1787

REVOLUTIONS

As to those mortal feuds, which in certain conjunctures spread a conflagration through a whole nation, or through a very large proportion of it, proceeding either from weighty causes of discontent given by the government, or from the contagion of some violent popular paroxism, they do not fall within any ordinary rules of calculation. When they happen, they commonly amount to revolutions and dismemberments of empire. No form of government can always either avoid or controul them. It is in vain to hope to guard against events too mighty for human insight or precaution, and it would be idle to object to a government because it could not perform impossibilities.
The Federalist No. 16, New York Packet,
4 December 1787

It was a thing hardly to be expected, that in a popular revolution the minds of men should stop at that happy mean, which marks the salutary boundary between *Power* and *Privilege*, and combines the energy of government with the security of private rights. A failure in the delicate and important point is the great source of the inconveniences we experience.
The Federalist No. 26, New York
Independent Journal, 22 December 1787

SACRIFICES

Great sacrifices ought to be made for a great object, but to make them or hazard them for an inferior object would be folly in the extreme.

To the Citizens . . . in the City of New York, New York, 22 April 1796

SELFISHNESS

A vast majority of mankind is entirely biased by motives of self-interest. Most men are glad to remove any burdens off themselves and place them upon the necks of their neighbors.

A Full Vindication of the Measures of Congress &c., New York, 15 December 1774

It is the temper of societies as well as of individuals to be impatient of constraint and to prefer partial [i.e., individual] to general interest.

The Continentalist No. II, New York Packet, 19 July 1781

SLANDER

I consider this spirit of abuse and calumny as the pest of society. I know the best of men are not exempt from the attacks of slander. . . . Drops of water, in long and continued succession, will wear out adamant.

Speech in People v. Croswell, Albany, N.Y., 14–15 February 1804

SOLITARY LEADERSHIP

There is always more decision, more dispatch, more secrecy, more responsibility where single men, than [where] bodies are concerned.

To Anthony Wayne, Morristown, N.J.,
28 December 1779

I proceed to lay it down as a rule, that one man of discernment is better fitted to analise and estimate the peculiar qualities adapted to particular offices, than a body of men of equal, or perhaps even of superior, discernment. . . . A single well directed man by a single understanding, cannot be distracted and warped by that diversity of views, feelings and interests, which frequently distracts and warp the resolutions of a collective body.

The Federalist No. 76, New York Packet,
1 April 1788

STEADINESS

Slow and sure is not a bad maxim. Snails are a wise generation.
To Theodore Sedgwick, New York, 27 February 1800

SYCOPHANCY

In Courts, sycophants flatter the errors & prejudices of the prince—in Republics sycophants flatter the errors and prejudices of the people. In both, honest and independent men are frequently obliged to tell unpalatable truths, which are well or ill received according to the virtue & good sense of those to whom they are addressed.

Philo Camilllus No. 3, New York Argus, 12 August 1795

TAKING THE INITIATIVE

It is also a common and well grounded rule in war to strike first.

To the New York Committee of Correspondence, Morristown, N.J., 5 April 1777

He who takes the first step, secures his debt.

Speech in the NewYork Ratifying Convention, 28 June 1788

TAXATION

There is perhaps nothing more likely to disturb the tranquility of nations, than their being bound to mutual contributions for any common object, which does not yield an equal and coincident benefit. For it is an observation as true, as it is trite, that there is nothing men differ so readily about as the payment of money.

The Federalist No. 7, New York Independent Journal, 17 November 1787

There is no part of the administration of government that requires extensive information and a thorough knowledge of the principles of political economy so much as the business of taxation. The man who understands these principles best will be least likely to resort to oppressive expedients, or to sacrifice any particular class of citizens to the procurement of revenue.

It might be demonstrated that the most productive system of finance will always be the least burthensome. There can be no doubt that in order to a judicious exercise of the power of taxation it is necessary that the person in whose hands it is should be acquainted with the general genius, habits and modes of thinking of the people at large and with the resources of the country.

The Federalist No. 35, New York Independent Journal, *5 January 1788*

Nations in general, even under governments of the more popular kind, usually commit the administration of their finances to single men or to boards composed of a few individuals, who digest and prepare, in the first instance, the plans of taxation, which are afterwards passed into laws by the authority of the sovereign or Legislature.

The Federalist No. 36, New York Packet, *8 January 1788*

The Question is very much What further taxes will be *least* unpopular?

To James Madison, New York, *12 October 1789*

TENURE

It is a general principle of human nature that a man will be interested in whatever he possesses, in proportion to the firmness or precariousness of the tenure, by which he holds it; will be less attached to what he holds by a momentary or uncertain title, than to what he enjoys by a durable or certain title; and of course will be willing to risk more for the sake of the one, than for the sake of the other.

The Federalist No. 71, New York Packet, *18 March 1788*

TRUTH

The best way of determining disputes and of investigating truth is by descending to elementary principles. Any other method may only bewilder and misguide the understanding.

"A Sincere Friend to America," The Farmer Refuted &c., *New York, 23 February 1775*

UNCERTAINTIES OF LIFE

The changes in the human condition are uncertain and frequent. Many, on whom fortune has bestowed her favours, may trace their family to a more unprosperous station; and many who are now in obscurity, may look back upon the affluence and exalted rank of their ancestors.

Speech in the New York Ratifying Convention, 28 June 1788

VANITY

With some men, the hardest thing to forgive is the demonstration of their errors—the manifestation that they are not infallible. Mortified vanity is one of the most corroding emotions of the human mind; one of the most inextinguishable sources of animosity and hatred.

The Vindication *No. I, Philadelphia, May–August 1792*

Vanity and jealousy exclude all counsel.

To Rufus King, New York, 5 January 1800

VIOLENCE

When the sword is once drawn, the passions of men observe no bounds of moderation.

The Federalist No. 16, New York Packet,
4 December 1787

WAR

Peace or war, will not always be left to our option; that however moderate or unambitious we may be, we cannot count upon the moderation, or hope to extinguish the ambition of others.

The Federalist No. 34, New York
Independent Journal, 5 January 1788

WEALTH

Is it not the love of wealth as domineering and enterprising a passion as that of power or glory?

The Federalist No. 6, New York
Independent Journal, 14 November 1787

ZEAL

It often happens that our zeal is at variance with our understanding.

To William Gordon, West Point, N.Y.,
5 September 1779

Biographical Notes

Adams, Abigail (Mass.): wife of John Adams
Adams, John (Mass.): lawyer, revolutionary, Continental Congress, signs Declaration of Independence, diplomat, first U.S. vice president, second U.S. president
Adams, John Quincy (Mass.): son of John Adams, U.S. senator, diplomat
Adams, Thomas Boylston (Mass.): son of John Adams, lawyer
Adgate, Jacob (N.Y.): farmer, mill owner, assembly, ratifying convention
Ames, Fisher (Mass.): lawyer, ratifying convention, U.S. representative
Bard, John (Pa.): physician
Barnwell, Robert (S.C.): planter, Continental Congress, state representative, ratifying convention, U.S. representative
Beckley, John (Va.): clerk Va. House of Delegates, ratifying convention, and U.S. House of Representatives; Jeffersonian political operative
Biddle, Charles (Pa.): Supreme Executive Council
Bland, Theodorick (Va.): planter, House of Delegates, ratifying convention, U.S. representative
Bogart, David S. (N.Y.): student at Columbia University, minister
Bradford, William (Pa.): lawyer, attorney general
Brissot de Warville (France): philosophe, traveler in U.S.
Burr, Aaron (N.Y.): N.Y. attorney general, U.S. senator, vice president under Jefferson, tried for treason, kills Hamilton in duel
Cabot, George (Mass.): merchant, U.S. senator
Church, Angelica Schuyler (N.Y., England): Hamilton's sister-in-law; in Jefferson's circle of friends
Clark, Abraham (N.J.): East Jersey party leader, Continental and Confederation Congress, signs Declaration of Independence, Annapolis Convention commissioner. U.S. representative
Clarkson, Matthew (N.Y.): merchant
Clinton, DeWitt (N.Y.): lawyer, son of James Clinton, nephew of George Clinton, party leader, mayor of New York City, presidential candidate
Clinton, George (N.Y.): lawyer, revolutionary, soldier, governor, president of ratifying convention, assembly, vice president under Jefferson and Madison
Clinton, James (N.Y.): soldier, brother of George Clinton, ratifying convention, state assembly and senate

Collins, John (R.I.): merchant, Confederation Congress, governor
Conway, Thomas (Ireland): soldier, cabal against George Washington
Coxe, Tench (Pa.): merchant, Federalist essayist, assistant secretary of the treasury, becomes Republican
DeSaussure, Henry W. (S.C.): director of U.S. Mint, diplomat
Dexter, Samuel (Mass.): lawyer, U.S. senator
Duer, William (N.Y.): merchant, financier, secretary to Confederation board of treasury, speculator, assistant secretary of treasury, bankrupt
Fenno, John (Pa.): printer *Gazette of the United States*
Ford, Mathew (N.Y.): assembly
Foster, Theodore (R.I.): Federalist, Providence town clerk, lawyer, merchant, historian, U.S. senator
Gates, Horatio (Va., N.Y.): soldier, president Board of War (Revolution), commands at Saratoga, defeated at Camden, S.C., cabal against Washington
Giles, William Branch (Va.): radical Republican leader in U.S. representative, U.S. senator
Gordon, William (England): minister, historian
Gore, Christopher (Mass.): lawyer, ratifying convention, U.S. district attorney for Mass., diplomat, governor, U.S. senator
Greene, Nathanael (R.I., Ga.): soldier, quartermaster general
Hamilton, Elizabeth Schuyler (N.Y.): Hamilton's wife; daughter of Philip Schuyler
Hancock, John (Mass.): merchant, revolutionary, president of Congress, governor, president ratifying convention
Hartley, Thomas (Pa.): lawyer, assembly, Council of Censors, ratifying convention, U.S. representative
Hazard, Nathaniel (N.Y.): merchant, former Loyalist
Heth, William (Va.): planter, Council of State, ratifying convention, collector of custom at Bermuda Hundred, Va.
Hughes, Hugh (N.Y.): teacher, deputy quartermaster general, Antifederalist essayist
Innes, James (Va.): lawyer, House of Delegates, state attorney general, ratifying convention
Jay, John (N.Y.): lawyer, delegate and president of Congress, diplomat, secretary for foreign affairs, co-author of The Federalist, ratifying convention, chief justice of the U.S., governor
Jefferson, Thomas (Va.): lawyer, planter, revolutionary, Continental and Confederation Congress, writes and signs Declaration of Independence, governor, diplomat, U.S. secretary of state, U.S. vice president, third U.S. president

Biographical Notes

Johnson, Robert C. (Conn.): lawyer, son of William Samuel Johnson
Johnston, Samuel (N.C.): lawyer, governor, ratifying convention (president), U.S. senator, presidential elector
Jones, Samuel (N.Y.): lawyer, Loyalist, Antifederalist, ratifying convention, codifies New York laws
Kent, James (N.Y.): lawyer; judge, chancellor of New York
King, Rufus (Mass., N.Y.): lawyer, Confederation Congress, Constitutional Convention, ratifying convention, U.S. senator, diplomat, vice presidential and presidential candidate
Knox, Henry (Mass.): bookseller, revolutionary, soldier, organizes Society of the Cincinnati, secretary at war
Knox, Hugh (St, Croix, West Indies): minister, teaches Hamilton
Kuhl, Henry (Pa.): clerk Confederation treasury, assistant cashier Bank of the United States
Lafayette, Marquis de (France): aristocrat, soldier, American Revolutionary general, lobbies in France for America
Lansing, John, Jr. (N.Y.): lawyer, Constitutional Convention, ratifying convention, mayor of Albany
Laurance, John (N.Y.): lawyer, U.S. representative, director Bank of the United States
Lee, Henry "Lighthorse Harry" (Va.): soldier, House of Delegates, Congress, ratifying convention, governor
Lenox, David (Pa.): U.S. marshal
Lowther, Tristram (N.Y.): Hamilton's fellow student at King's College
Maclay, William (Pa.): U.S. senator, keeps personal journal while in Senate
Madison, James (Va.): planter, Confederation Congress, Va. House of Delegates, Constitutional Convention, ratifying convention, co-author The Federalist, member U.S. representative, U.S. secretary of state, fourth U.S. president
Malcolm, William (N.Y.): soldier, receiver of Continental taxes, assembly
Marshall, Thomas (Mass.): soldier
McGregor, Collin (N.Y.): merchant, financial broker
McHenry, James (Md.): physician, soldier, aide to Washington, Constitutional Convention, ratifying convention, U.S. secretary of war
Miller, Henry (Pa.): supervisor of revenue for Pa.
Monroe, James (Va.): planter, soldier, Confederation Congress, ratifying convention, diplomat, fifth U.S. president
Morris, Gouverneur (N.Y., Pa.): lawyer, large land owner, delegate to Congress, assistant superintendent of finance, Constitutional Convention, diplomat, U.S. senator

Morris, Richard (N.Y.): lawyer, chief justice of N.Y. supreme court, ratifying convention

Morris, Robert (Pa.): merchant, Continental Congress, signs Declaration of Independence, superintendent of finance, Constitutional Convention, U.S. senator, bankrupt

Morse, Jedidiah (Conn.): minister, geographer

Moustier, Comte de (France): diplomat, minister to U.S.

Nicholas, John (Va.): U.S. representative

North, William (N.Y.): soldier, adjutant general, son-in-law of James Duane

Nourse, Joseph (N.Y., Pa., Washington, D.C.): register of treasury (Confederation and U.S.)

Olney, Jeremiah (R.I.): soldier, collector of customs, Providence

Otto, Louis-Guillaume (France): diplomat, charge d'affaires

Paine, Ephraim (N.Y.): state senator

Pendleton, Nathaniel (Ga.): lawyer, aide de camp to Nathanael Greene, U.S. district judge

Pickering, Timothy (Pa., Mass.): quartermaster general, postmaster general, assistant secretary of the treasury, U.S. secretary of state

Pierce, William (Ga.): merchant, soldier, Confederation Congress, Constitutional Convention, wrote sketches of delegates

Pinckney, Charles Cotesworth (S.C.): lawyer/planter, Constitutional Convention, assembly, ratifying convention, diplomat, presidential candidate

Pinckney, Thomas (S.C.): governor, president of ratifying convention, diplomat presidential candidate

Platt, Richard (N.Y.): broker, speculator, bankrupt

Platt, Zephaniah (N.Y.): farmer, flour mill owner, state senator, judge, ratifying convention

Plumer, William (N.H.): lawyer, U.S. senator

Putnam, Israel (Conn.): soldier

Randolph, Edmund (Va.): lawyer, Va. attorney general, governor, Constitutional Convention, ratifying convention, U.S. attorney general, U.S. secretary of state

Rittenhouse, David (Pa.): scientist, inventor, treasurer

Rush, Benjamin (Pa.): physician, social reformer, Continental Congress, signs Declaration of Independence, ratifying convention

Rutledge, John (S.C.): lawyer, revolutionary, governor, Constitutional Convention, ratifying convention, U.S. supreme court, S. C. chief justice, U.S. chief justice (not confirmed)

Biographical Notes

Rutledge, John, Jr. (S.C.): U.S. Representative, presidential elector
Scott, John Morin (N.Y.): soldier, Continental Congress, lawyer, N.Y. supreme court
Schuyler, Philip (N.Y.): wealthy landowner, revolutionary, assembly, soldier, state senator, U.S. senator, Hamilton's father-in-law
Shippen, Thomas Lee (Pa.): student, lawyer
Smith, Melancton (N.Y.): merchant, Clintonian leader, delegate Congress, Antifederalist essayist, ratifying convention (Antifederalist manager)
Smith, William Loughton (S.C.): lawyer, U.S. representative
Smith, William (Md.): merchant
Smith, William Stephens (N.Y.): soldier, diplomat, son-in-law of John Adams
Stanton, Joseph, Jr. (R.I.): soldier, wealthy farmer, leader of Antifederalists, ratifying convention, U.S. senator, U.S. representative
Steuben, Baron Fredrich Wilhelm von (Prussia, N.Y.): soldier
Stoddert, Benjamin (Md.): merchant, Rev. Board of War, secretary of the navy
Sullivan, John (N.H.): lawyer, miller, soldier, Congress, attorney general, president (governor), ratifying convention (president), U.S. district judge
Tillinghast, Charles (N.Y.): distiller, deputy collector of custom for New York City, son-in-law of John Lamb, secretary of New York Federal Republican Committee
Tredwell, Thomas (N.Y.): lawyer, probate judge, assembly, state senator, ratifying convention, U.S. representative
Troup, Robert (N.Y.): lawyer, assembly, clerk of U.S. district court
Trumbull, John (Conn.): soldier, aide to Washington
Van Cortlandt, Pierre (N.Y.): large landowner, lieutenant governor
Verplank, Gulian (N.Y.): president Bank of New York
Warren, Mercy Otis (Mass.): playwright, poet, historian, wife of James Warren, close friend of John and Abigail Adams
Washington, George (Va.): planter, revolutionary, soldier, U.S. commander in chief, president Constitutional Convention, first U.S. president, commander in chief of U.S. provisional army
Webb, Samuel Blachley (N.Y.): soldier, merchant
Wheelock, John (N.H.): president of Dartmouth College
Wilkinson, James (Md., New Orleans): soldier, intriguer
Wolcott, Oliver, Jr. (Conn.) lawyer, treasury officer, U.S. secretary of the treasury

Wolcott, Oliver, Sr. (Conn.): Continental Congress, signs Declaration of Independence and Articles of Confederation, judge, lieutenant governor, governor

Yates, Abraham, Jr. (N.Y.): cobbler, revolutionary, state senator, Antifederalist essayist, mayor of Albany

Yates, Robert (N.Y.): lawyer, revolutionary, N.Y. supreme court; Constitutional Convention, ratifying convention, Federalist candidate for governor

Index

Adams, Abigail, xx; id., 205; describes AH, 45, 50–51, 55–56, 60; receives letter describing AH, 46, 49–52

Adams, Charles: receives letter describing AH, 50–51

Adams, John, xx, 52–53, 58, 76, 120; id., 205; describes AH, 28, 31, 46, 49–50, 60–62, 66–72, 77–81; described by AH, 85–89; receives letter describing AH, 28, 45, 50, 53–56, 71–73; receives letters from AH, 107, 155–57, 179, 180

Adams, John Quincy: id., 205; describes AH, 62

Adams, Samuel, 62

Adams, Thomas Boylston: id., 205; describes AH, 51–52; receives letter describing AH, 51, 61–62

Address and Strategy, 165

Administration, 165

Adgate, Jacob: id., 205; described by AH, 90

"Adrastus": describes AH, 13

Adversity, 165

Albany Supervisors: receive letter from AH, 161–62

Alien and Sedition Laws, 70

Ambition, 3, 10, 11, 35, 54, 59, 60, 65, 67, 70, 76, 78, 82, 91, 94, 95, 98–103, 118, 119, 153, 157, 166, 181, 194, 203

Ames, Fisher, 50; id., 205; describes AH, 25

Appearances, 166

Argumentation, 166

Aurora (Philadelphia), describes AH, 57

Bad Men, 166

Bard, John: id., 205; describes AH, 35–36

Barlow, Joel: receives letter describing AH, 73

Barnwell, Robert: id., 205; described by AH, 90

Barrell, Joseph: receives letter describing AH, 16

Bayard, James A: receives letters from AH, 93, 96–97, 100–103, 121–22, 166, 192

Beckley, John: id., 205; describes AH, 59

Benton, Egbert, 82

Biddle, Charles: id., 205; described by AH, 90–91

Black, Moses, 50

Black Soldiers, 3–4, 135

Bland, Theodorick: id., 205; described by AH, 91

Bogart, David S.: id., 205; describes AH, 17

Boldness, 166. *See also* Initiative; Taking the initiative

Boston Patriot: descriptions of AH, 72, 78–80

Boudinot, Elias: receives letter from AH, 151–52
Bradford, William: id., 205; describes AH, 48
Brevity, 167
Brissot de Warville: id., 205; describes AH, 21–22
British Constitution, 74, 75
Burr, Aaron, xxi, 32; id., 205; described by AH, xx, 91–103

Cabot, George, 50; id., 205; describes AH, 54, 60, 66
Candor, 21, 81
Carrington, Edward, 46; receives letter describing AH, 33–35; receives letters from AH, 90, 114, 118, 125, 131, 179, 191
Carroll, Charles of Carrollton: receives letters from AH, 86–87
Channing, William: describes AH, 29
Character, 3, 20, 38, 94, 96
Christian Fortitude, 167. *See also* Firmness; Perseverance
Church, Angelic Schuyler: id., 205; describes AH, 27; receives letter describing AH, 15; receives letters from AH, 125, 149
"A Citizen, and Real Friend to Order and Good Government," 17
Clark, Abraham: id., 205; describes AH, 24
Clarkson, Matthew: id., 205; described by AH, 103
Clinton, Cornelia: receives letter describing AH, 37
Clinton, DeWitt: id., 205; describes AH, 37

Clinton, George, xv, xvii, xix, 22, 91, 127, 143; id., 205; describes AH, 18; described by AH, 103–8; receives letter from AH, 108
Clinton, James: id., 205; described by AH, 108
Collins, John: id., 206; described by AH, 108
Colt, Peter: receives letter from AH, 134
Commerce, 167
Conformity, 167
Constitutional Convention, xvi–xvii
Constitution Making, 168. *See also* First principles
Controlling Events, 168
Conway, Thomas, 23; described by AH, 108
Coxe, Tench: id., 206; described by AH, 109–10
Cranch, Mary: receives letter describing AH, 60
Cruger, Nicholas, xiii

Dane, Nathan: receives letter describing AH, 18–19
Dayton, Jonathan: receives letter describing AH, 24; receives letters from AH, 166, 178, 195
Death, 4
Deception, 168
Deference, 169–70
Demagogues, 34, 170
DeSaussure, Henry W.: id., 206; described by AH, 110
Dexter, Samuel: id., 206; described by AH, 110–11
Discretion, 6, 73, 75, 76, 143, 170–71
Dissemble, 6

Index

Divide and Conquer, 171
Doing What Is Right, 171
Duane, James: receives letters from AH, 112–13, 126, 129, 149
Dueling, 64, 65
Duer, William, 69; id., 206; described by AH, 111
Dutch Bankers: receive letter from AH, 159–60
Duty, 37, 57, 171

Economy, 46
Elections, 172
Emergencies, 172
Enemies, 173
Example, 173
Exaggerations, 173
Excise Taxes, 173. *See also* Taxation
Executive Power, 174
Experience, 174

Factions, 56–57, 175. *See also* Political parties
False Information, 175
Federalism, 175–76
Fenner, Arthur: receives letter describing AH, 32
Fenno, John: id., 206; describes AH, 26–27
Finding a Husband, 176
Finding a Wife, 177
Firmness, 177. *See also* Christian fortitude; Perseverance
First Principles, 177. *See also* Constitution making
Ford, Mathew: id., 206; described by AH, 90
Foster, Theodore: id., 206; describes AH, 32; receives letter describing AH, 29

France, 23, 42, 101, 118, 122, 177–78
Franklin, Benjamin, 87
Fraunces, Andrew G.: receives letter describing AH, 37

Gambling, 178
Gates, Horatio, 36, 152; id., 206; described by AH, 112–13
General Surmises, 178
Giles, William Branch, 46; id., 206; described by AH, 114
Glory, 4, 9, 65, 75, 82, 102, 166, 203. *See also* Honor
Godwin, William, 100, 103
Good with the Bad, 178
Gordon, William: id., 206; described by AH, 114–15; receives letters from AH, 115, 171, 203
Gore, Christopher: id., 206; described by AH, 110–11; receives letter describing AH, 64
Gossip, 156, 179. *See also* Slander
Government, 179–80. *See also* Constitution making; First principles; Laws; Solitary leadership
Greene, Nathanael: id., 206; described by AH, 115

Half-Confidence, 155, 157, 180
Hamilton, Alexander: describes himself, 3–10, 12, 15, 29, 33–37, 41, 44, 45, 48, 49, 54–58, 62–65; receives letter describing AH, 5–6, 7–8, 10–11, 11, 26, 27, 29, 32, 33, 35–36, 45–49, 56–61; as a colossus, 48
"An American," 119
"Cæsar," xvii, 169–70, 170
"Camillus," 48

"Cattullus," 119
To the Citizens in the City of New York, 198
"The Continentalist," xvi, 138, 188–89, 193, 198
The Defence of the Funding System, 166, 171, 173, 181
Defence of the President's Neutrality Proclamation, 153, 187, 195
To the Electors of the State of New York, 162
Eulogy on Nathanael Greene, xv, 25, 115, 165, 166, 192
The Farmer Refuted, 3, 185, 186, 202
A Full Vindication of Congress, 3, 166, 187–88, 198
General Orders, 1800, 178
"Hambden," 121
"H.G." Letters, 106–7, 173, 182, 190
Letter Concerning the Public Conduct and Character of John Adams, 59–61, 88–89, 142–43, 154
To the New York Committee of Correspondence, 200
Quebec Bill Remarks, 183
"Philo-Camillus," 199–200
"Phocion," 21, 181, 184, 187
"Publius," The Federalist, xviii, xxii, 15, 16, 18, 19, 21–23, 165, 167, 168, 171, 172–78, 180–82, 184–97, 199–203
Speeches in Constitutional Convention, 181
Speech in New York Assembly, 12
Speeches in Ratification Convention, xviii–xix, 17–20, 21, 24, 178, 183, 200, 202
Speech in People v. Croswell, 198
The Vindication, 202
"The Warning," *Gazette of the United States*, 188
Washington's Farewell Address Draft, xix, 183

Hamilton, Elizabeth Schuyler, xv, 4; id., 206; described by AH, 115–16; receives letters describing AH, 9, 12, 54–55, 57, 65, 81–82; receives letters from AH, 113, 116, 146, 167, 180
Hamilton, James A.: receives letters from AH, 170–71, 171
Hancock, John, 662, 85; id., 206; described by AH, 116–17
Happiness, 180
Harper, Robert G.: receives letter from AH, 127–28
Harrison, Robert Hanson: receives letters from AH, 91, 127–28
Harsh Words, 181
Hartley, Thomas: id., 206; describes AH, 28
Hazard, Nathaniel: id., 206; describes AH, 33
Heth, William: id., 206; describes AH, 45–46, 48–49
History, 193
Hoffman, Josiah Ogden: receives letter describing AH, 56–57
Hogeboom, Catherine: receives letter describing AH, 18
Honesty, 181. *See also* Integrity
Honor, 10, 14, 27, 181. *See also* Glory
Hughes, Hugh: id., 206; describes AH, 15–16
Human Nature, 181–82
Hypocrisy, 49, 50, 115, 121, 133

Index

Imagination, 182
Immigration, 183
Indifference, 183
Industry and Frugality, 183
Ingenuity, 183
Initiative, 166, 184. *See also* Boldness; Taking the initiative
Innes, James: id., 206; described by AH, 117
"Inspector": describes AH, 13–14
Integrity, 16, 19, 20, 23, 27, 32, 35, 54, 60, 62, 70, 88, 92, 93, 105, 106, 120, 126, 138. *See also* Honesty
Intolerance, 184
Intrigue, 28, 43, 45–46, 46, 49, 50, 51, 57, 71, 93, 98, 109, 119, 132, 184
Iredell, James: receives letters describing AH, 24, 27

Jackson, Jonathan: described by AH, 117
Jackson, William: receives letter describing AH, 58
Jamieson, Neil: receives letter describing AH, 16
Jay, John, xviii, 107; id., 206; described by AH, 117–18; receives letter describing AH, 10; receives letters from AH, 117–18, 120–21, 123, 132–33
Jealousy, 185
Jefferson, Thomas, xix, 32, 33, 35, 57–58, 95, 102, 131; id., 206; describes AH, 37, 48, 73, 74; described by AH, xx, 118–22; receives letters describing AH, 24, 80–81
Johnson, Robert C.: id., 207; describes AH, 18

Johnson, William Samuel, xvii, 33; receives letter describing AH, 18
Johnston, Samuel: id., 207; describes AH, 27
Jones, Samuel: id., 207; described by AH, 122–23
Judiciary, 185

Kent, James: id., 207; describes AH, 15, 20–21, 81–82, 82
King, Rufus: id., 207; describes AH, 64; described by AH, 123–25; receives letters describing AH, 61, 63, 63–64; receives letters from AH, 86, 107, 120, 137, 145, 154, 171, 178, 191, 202
Kirby, Ephraim: receives letter describing AH, 59
Knox, Henry, 46, 54; id., 207; described by AH, 125; receives letter describing AH, 56
Knox, Hugh, xiii; id., 207; describes AH, 11
Kuhl, Henry: id., 207; described by AH, 126

Labor, 185
Lafayette, Marquis de, 23; id., 207; describes AH, 5, 5–6; described by AH, 126–27; receives letter describing AH, 10; receives letter from AH, 127
Lamb, John: receives letters describing AH, 17, 18
Langdon, John: receives letter describing AH, 30
Lansing, John, Jr., xvi; id., 207; described by AH, 127–28
Laurance, John: id., 207; described by AH, 128
Laurens, John: receives letters

describing AH, 4–6; receives
letters from AH, 112, 114, 116,
134–35, 165, 177, 187, 188
Lawrence, Nathaniel: receives letter describing AH, 15
Laws, 185. *See also* Government
Leadership, 186. *See also* Solitary leadership
Lear, Tobias: receives letter from AH, 153–54
Ledyard, Isaac: receives letter from AH, 184
Lee, Henry "Lighthorse Harry": id., 207; described by AH, 128, 188
Lee, Richard Henry, 85
Lenox, David: id., 207; described by AH, 128–29
Letter from Boston: describes AH, 31
Letter from New York: describes AH, 24–25
Liberty, 186
Livingston, Philip: receives letters from AH, 188
Livingston, Robert R., 32, 101; receives letters from AH, 90, 104, 145–46, 173
Livingston, Susanna: receives letter describing AH, 35; receives letter from AH, 104
Livingston, Walter: receives letter from AH, 111
Livingston, William: receives letter from AH, 148–49
Love, 186
Lowell, John: receives letters describing AH, 25, 66
Lowther, Tristram: id., 207; describes AH, 24
Loyalists, 61, 68
Luzerne, Marquis de la, 23, 135

Maclay, William: id., 207; describes AH, 28
McGregor, Collin: id., 207; describes AH, 16
Madison, James, xviii, xix, 21, 32, 33, 35, 118; id., 207; described by AH, 131; receives letters describing AH, 22, 37, 48; receives letters from AH, 85, 105–6, 125, 201
McHenry, James: id., 207; describes AH, 10–11, 26, 47, 57, 59, 76–77; described by AH, 129–31; receives letter describing AH, 6–7; receives letters from AH, 86, 99–100, 155, 191
McKean, Thomas, 62
Malcolm, William: id., 207; described by AH, 131–33
Marriage, 4, 11, 22, 23, 176, 177
Marshall, Thomas: id., 207; described by AH, 134
Merit, 187
Mifflin, Thomas: receives letter from AH, 172
Military Training, 187
Miller, Henry: id., 207; described by AH, 134
Mischief, 187
Mistakes, 187–88
Moderation, 188, 203
Monarchy, 34–35, 69, 76, 78
Money, 188, 196. *See also* Taxation
Monroe, James: id., 207; describes AH, 41–44; described by AH, 134–35
Montmorin, Comte de: receives letters describing AH, 26, 29
Morris, Gouverneur, 40; id., 207; describes AH, 61, 63, 69, 75–76;

Index

described by AH, 135–37; receives letter describing AH, 62–63; receives letters from AH, 95

Morris, Richard: id., 208; described by AH, 137

Morris, Robert, 9, 82; id., 208; described by AH, 137–39; receives letter describing AH, 9; receives letters from AH, 104–5, 127, 128, 133, 137–38, 141, 143, 146–47, 150, 160, 161, 178, 185

Morse, Jedidiah: id., 208; describes AH, 59–60

Moustier, Comte de: id., 208; describes AH, 26

National Government for America, 188–89

National Security, 189–90

Neglects and Slights, 190

Neutrality, 190

New York City Citizens: receive letter from AH,

New York Committee of Correspondence: receives letter from AH, 200

New York State Electors: receive letter from AH, 162

Nicholas, John: id., 208; describes AH, 37–41

Nichols, Francis: described by AH, 128–29

Noailles, Vicomte de: receives letter from AH, 177

North, William: id., 208; describes AH, 58

Nourse, Joseph: id., 208; described by AH, 139

Obstinacy, 105, 106, 141, 190
Officeholders, 191

Ogden, Dr.: receives letters describing AH, 60–61, 69

Olney, Jeremiah: id., 208; described by AH, 140–41; receives letter describing AH, 36–37; receives letters from AH, 108, 140–41

Oratory (eloquence), 12–13, 17, 20, 21, 23, 25, 49

Otis, Harrison Gray: receives letter from AH, 94–95

Otto, Louis-Guillaume: id., 208; describes AH, 22–23, 29

Overlooking Faults, 191

Paine, Ephraim: id., 208; described by AH, 141

Passions, 35, 89, 118, 133, 191–92, 203

Peale Charles Willson, 11

Pendleton, Nathaniel: id., 208; described by AH, 141–42

Perseverance, 11, 115, 187. *See also* Christian fortitude; Firmness

Pessimism, 5

Peters, Richard: receives letter describing AH, 64

Pickering, Timothy, 130; id., 208; describes AH, 52–53; described by AH, 142; receives letters describing AH, 54, 76–77; receives letters from AH, 86, 109, 123, 128, 141–42

Pierce, William: id., 208; id., 208; describes AH, 12–13

Pinckney, Charles Cotesworth, xx, 50; id., 208; described by AH, 142; receives letters from AH, 92, 119, 147, 168, 172

Pinckney, Thomas, xx, 86, 87, 120;

id., 208; described by AH, 142–43
Platt, Richard: describes AH, 20
Platt, Zephaniah: id., 208; described by AH, 143
Plumer, William, xi; id., 208; describes AH, 70, 103
Poetry, 36; describing AH, 14–15
Political Mobility, 192
Political Parties, 42, 192. See also Factions
Pope, Alexander, 36
Power, 9, 34, 75, 78–79, 95, 96, 98, 176, 193–94, 196–97, 197, 203
Promotion, 195
Public Esteem, 195
Public Opinion, 195
Putnam, Israel: id., 208; described by AH, 143–44; receives letters from AH, 103–4, 108, 131–32

Randolph, Edmund: id., 208; describes AH, 22; described by AH, 144
Religion, 73–74, 118, 121, 187
Republican Principles, 10, 33, 75. See also First principles
Responsibility in Office, 196
Revenue, 196–97. See also Taxation
Revolutions, 197
Rittenhouse, David: id., 208; described by AH, 144
Ross, James: receives letter from AH, 98–99
Rush, Benjamin: id., 208; describes AH, 66, 71–72; receives letters describing AH, 67–71, 74, 78
Russell, Thomas: describes AH, 30
Rutledge, John: id., 208; described by AH, 145–46

Rutledge, John, Jr.: id., 209; describes AH, 58

Sacrifices, 198
Sargent, Winthrop: receives letter describing AH, 20
Schuyler, Elizabeth. See Hamilton, Elizabeth Schuyler
Schuyler, John Bradstreet: receives letter describing AH, 17
Schuyler, Margarita: receives letters from AH, 115–16, 176, 186
Schuyler, Philip, xv, 27; id., 209; describes AH, 7–8, 17; described by AH, 145–46; receives letter from AH, 152–53
Scott, John Morin: id., 209; described by AH, 146–47
Seabury, Samuel, 3
Sedgwick, Theodore: receives letters describing AH, 30, 31; receives letters from AH, 85, 94, 116–17, 199
Selfishness, 198
Seton, Hugh: receives letters from AH, 91, 122–23
Shippen, Thomas Lee: id., 209; describes AH, 24
Slander, 56–57, 198. See also Gossip
Slavery, xvi
Smith, Melancton: id., 209; describes AH, 18–19
Smith, William Loughton, 50; id., 209; described by AH, 147
Smith, William: id., 209; describes AH, 25
Smith, William Stephens, 55; id., 209; described by AH, 147–48
Solitary Leadership, 199
"A Spectator," 24

Stanton, Joseph, Jr.: id., 209; describes AH, 32
Steadiness, 199
Steele, John: receives letters from AH, 86, 92–93, 108, 120
Sterne, Laurance, 8
Steuben, Baron Fredrich Wilhelm von: id., 209; described by AH, 148–49
Stevens, Edward: receives letter describing AH, 3
Stewart, Walter: receives letter describing AH, 29
Stoddert, Benjamin: id., 209; describes AH, 72–73
Sullivan, John: id., 209; describes AH, 9, 30; receives letter describing AH, 6
Swan, Caleb: receives letter from AH, 167
Sycophancy, 199–200

Taking the Initiative, 200. See also Initiative.
Taxation, 200–201. See also Excise tax; Revenue
Tenure, 201
Thatcher, George: receives letter from AH, 117
Tillinghast, Charles: id., 209; describes AH, 17
Timidity, 37
Tredwell, Thomas: id., 209; described by AH, 150
Troup, Robert: id., 209; describes AH, 32, 61, 63, 63–64, 73; described by AH, 150; receives letter describing AH, 48
Trumbull, John, x; id., 209; describes AH, 27, 28; receives letters describing AH, 28, 31
Truth, 202

Uncertainties of Life, 202
Upward Mobility, xiii, xv, xxii, 192

Van Cortlandt, Pierre: id., 209; described by AH, 150
Vanity, 13, 27, 60, 67, 87, 89, 120, 132, 133, 202
Vans Murray, William: receives letter describing AH, 62
Van Schaack, Henry: describes AH, 30, 31
Verplank, Gulian: id., 209; described by AH, 151
Violence, 203

Wadsworth, Jeremiah: receives letter from AH, 120
Walsh, Robert: receives letter describing AH, 75–76
War, xiv, 3, 203
Ward, Joseph: receives letters describing AH, 26–27, 72
Warren, Mercy Otis: id., 209; describes AH, 151; receives letter from AH, 151
Washington, George, xiv, xvii, 7–8, 17, 22, 39, 40, 62, 71–72, 104; id., 209; describes AH, 6, 46–47, 53–54; described by AH, 151–54; receives letters describing AH, 5, 9, 35, 37–49, 52–53; receives letters from AH, 90–91, 103, 109–11, 117, 118, 123–25, 128–31, 134, 135–44, 147–48, 148, 150, 154–55, 157–59, 168, 181, 195
Waterhouse, Benjamin: receives letter describing AH, 77–78
Wayne, Anthony, 156; receives letter from AH, 199
Wealth, 203

Webb, Samuel Blachley, 28; id., 209; describes AH, 16, 18; receives letter describing AH, 17

Wheelock, John: id., 209; describes AH, 29

Wilkinson, James: id., 209; describes AH, 56; described by AH, 154–57

Williams, Otho H.: receives letter describing AH, 25

Willing, Thomas: receives letter from AH, 126

Wilson, James: receives letter from AH, 167

Wolcott, Elizabeth: receives letter describing AH, 26

Wolcott, Oliver, Jr., 69; id., 209; describes AH, 26; described by AH, 157–60; receives letter describing AH, 27, 59–60; receives letters from AH, 93, 93–94, 110, 129–30, 142, 148, 151, 160, 177

Wolcott, Oliver, Sr.: id., 210; describes AH, 27

Women, 15, 35, 187. *See also* Marriage

Yates, Abraham, Jr.: id., 210; described by AH, 160

Yates, Robert, xvi; id., 210; described by AH, 161–62

Yeates, Jasper: receives letter describing AH, 28

Zeal, 141, 184, 188, 193, 194, 203

About the Author

John Kaminski earned the PhD from the University of Wisconsin–Madison in 1972. He has worked on The Documentary History of the Ratification of the Constitution series since 1969, first as associate editor and, beginning in 1980, as director. Twenty-seven volumes of this magisterial work have been published by the Wisconsin Historical Society Press and the electronic version has been placed on the University of Virginia's "Rotunda" and the University of Wisconsin–Madison Libraries website. In 1981 he founded and continues to direct The Center for the Study of the American Constitution (CSAC) in the Department of History at the University of Wisconsin–Madison.

In addition to the *Ratification* series, Kaminski has edited, co-edited, or written twenty-six other books, as well as many articles on the Revolutionary era, with special emphasis on the Constitution, the Bill of Rights, the judiciary, slavery, and the Founding Fathers, including George Washington, Thomas Jefferson, James Madison, John Jay, Thomas Paine, the Marquis de Lafayette, and John and Abigail Adams. He has spoken on these subjects throughout the country and abroad. He has appeared on Wisconsin Public Radio almost thirty times; audio and video of these appearances are available free on the CSAC's website. He referees manuscripts for scholarly journals and presses, and serves on panels for several federal government funding agencies.

In 1994, Kaminski instituted a judicial education program in conjunction with the Wisconsin Office of Judicial Education. Between 1995 and 2013 this program expanded to include over 150 one-day seminars for federal judges through the auspices of the Federal Judicial Center, and from 1997 through 2010 Kaminski served on the visiting faculty of the National Judicial College in Reno, Nevada. Through the use of historical documents, the CSAC's judicial seminars gave judges the opportunity to learn about the historical beginnings of America with emphasis on the nation's philosophical underpinnings.

Kaminski and his wife of almost fifty years live in Middleton, Wisconsin. Their daughter, an urban planner, lives in San Francisco, and their son and daughter-in-law, both accountants, live in Sun Prairie, Wisconsin, with their two sons, both in middle school.